$GML:
The Billion Dollar Secret

⟨!CFG OIM⟩ The Charles F. Goldfarb Series on Open Information Management

"Open Information Management" (OIM) means managing information so that it is open to processing by any program, not just the program that created it. That extends even to application programs not conceived of at the time the information was created.

OIM is based on the principle of data independence: data should be stored in computers in non-proprietary, genuinely standardized representations. And that applies even when the data is the content of a document. Its representation should distinguish the innate information from the proprietary codes of document processing programs and the artifacts of particular presentation styles.

Business data bases—which rigorously separate the real data from the input forms and output report—achieved data independence decades ago. But documents, unlike business data, have historically been created in the context of a particular output presentation style. So for document data, independence was largely unachievable until recently.

That is doubly unfortunate. It is unfortunate because documents are a far more significant repository of humanity's information. And documents can contain significantly richer information structures than data bases.

It is also unfortunate because the need for OIM of documents is greater now than ever. The demands of "repurposing" require that information be deliverable in multiple formats (paper-based, online, multimedia, hypermedia). And information must now be delivered through multiple channels (traditional bookstores and libraries, online services, the Internet).

Fortunately, in the past ten years a technology has emerged that extends to documents the data base's capacity for data independence. And it does so without the data base's restrictions on structural freedom. That technology is the "Standard Generalized Markup Language" (SGML), an official International Standard (ISO 8879) that has been adopted by the world's largest producers of documents.

With SGML, organizations in government, aerospace, airlines, automotive, electronics, computers, and publishing (to name a few) have freed their documents from hostage relationships to processing software. SGML coexists with other data standards needed for OIM and acts as the framework that relates objects in the other formats to one another and to SGML documents.

As the enabling standard for OIM of documents, SGML necessarily plays a leading role in this series. We provide tutorials on SGML and other key standards and the techniques for applying them. Our books are not addressed solely to technical readers; we cover topics like the business justification for OIM and the business aspects of commerce in electronic information. We share the practical experience of organizations and individuals who have applied the techniques of OIM in environments ranging from immense industrial publishing projects to self-publishing on the World Wide Web.

Our authors are expert practitioners in their subject matter, not writers hired to cover a "hot" topic. They bring insight and understanding that can only come from real-world experience. Moreover, they practice what they preach about standardization. Their books share a common standards-based vocabulary. In this way, knowledge gained from one book in the series is directly applicable when reading another, or the standards themselves. This is just one of the ways in which we strive for the utmost technical accuracy and consistency with the OIM standards.

And we also strive for a sense of excitement and fun. After all, the challenge of OIM—preserving information from the ravages of technology while exploiting its benefits—is one of the great intellectual adventures of our age. I'm sure you'll find this series to be a knowledgable and reliable guide on that adventure.

About the Series Editor

Dr. Charles F. Goldfarb is the inventor of SGML and HyTime, and technical leader of the committees that developed them into International Standards. He is an information management consultant based in Saratoga, CA.

About the Series Logo

The rebus is an ancient literary tradition, dating from 16th century Picardy, and is especially appropriate to a series involving fine distinctions between things and the words that describe them. For the logo, Andrew Goldfarb, who also designed the series' "Intelligent Icons," incorporated a rebus of the series name within a stylized SGML comment declaration.

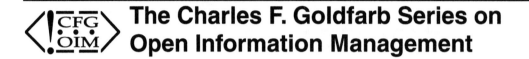
The Charles F. Goldfarb Series on Open Information Management

Turner, Douglass, and Turner *README.1ST: SGML for Writers and Editors*

Donovan *Industrial-Strength SGML: An Introduction to Enterprise Publishing*

Ensign *$GML: The Billion Dollar Secret*

$GML:
The Billion Dollar Secret

Chet Ensign

Prentice Hall PTR
Upper Saddle River, New Jersey 07458
http://www.prenhall.com

Editorial/production supervision: *Eileen Clark*
Composition: *Ronnie Bucci*
Cover design director: *Jerry Votta*
Cover design: *Talar Agasyon*
Manufacturing manager: *Alexis R. Heydt*
Marketing manager: *Dan Rush*
Acquisitions editor: *Mark L. Taub*
Editorial assistant: *Kate Hargett*

© 1997 by Prentice Hall PTR
Prentice-Hall, Inc.
A Simon & Schuster Company
Upper Saddle River, New Jersey 07458

The publisher offers discounts on this book when ordered in bulk quantities.
For more information, contact:

    Corporate Sales Department, Prentice Hall PTR
    One Lake Street, Upper Saddle River, NJ 07458
    Phone: 800-382-3419; FAX: 201- 236-7141
    E-mail: corpsales@prenhall.com

Printed in the United States of America
10 9 8 7 6 5 4 3 2 1

ISBN 0-13-226705-5

Prentice-Hall International (UK) Limited, *London*
Prentice-Hall of Australia Pty. Limited, *Sydney*
Prentice-Hall Canada Inc., *Toronto*
Prentice-Hall Hispanoamericana, S.A., *Mexico*
Prentice-Hall of India Private Limited, *New Delhi*
Prentice-Hall of Japan, Inc., *Tokyo*
Simon & Schuster Asia Pte. Ltd., *Singapor*
Editora Prentice-Hall do Brasil, Ltda., *Rio de Janeiro*

Contents

FIGURES . . . . **XV**

FOREWORD . . . . **XVII**

INTRODUCTION . . . . **XIX**

        Introduction: A Book for Executives xix

        Why "the Billion Dollar Secret"? xx

        How the Book Is Organized xxii

        Acknowledgments xxiv

CHAPTER 1   **THE COTTAGE INDUSTRY**
                RIGHT UNDER YOUR NOSE **1**

        Document-Based Information
        Is Crucial to Your Company 6

        The Productivity Dilemma
        with Documents 10

        Writing Document-Based Information:
        The New Cottage Industry 15

        Computers Can Perform Miracles —
        When They Have the Right Data 17

        Today's "Documents" Are Not "Data" 19

        From Documents to Information:
        Enter SGML, the Standard
        Generalized Markup Language 22

CHAPTER 2 **BUILDING CUTTING-EDGE INFORMATION PRODUCTS FROM DOCUMENTS — WHY IT DOESN'T WORK TODAY** 27

Taking On a Business Challenge 28

Electronic Documents — The Publishing Panacea? 29

The Lessons of the Prototype 31

TIMS Gets Real 33

Getting to the Source of the Matter 33

The Trouble with Text 35

The 101st-Page Paradox 37

What Went Wrong? 39

CHAPTER 3 **GROLIER, INCORPORATED** 43

The Original Database: Grolier, Incorporated 45

The Business Challenge 46

Publishing the "Original Database" 48

More Than a Hardware Problem 51

Understanding the Process 52

And Defining the Objectives 55

Why SGML? 56

Taking the Objectives to the Manufacturers . . . 58

Converting 27,000 Pages to SGML 59

Implementing the System 61

The Payoff 62

CHAPTER 4   SYBASE, INCORPORATED **71**

The Saga of Sybooks™:
Sybase, Incorporated   73

The Business Challenge   74

A Corporate Commitment to Standards   76

Changing the Way Information Is Delivered . .   78

A Rainbow of Online Publishing Solutions . . .   79

The Solution Is in the Data   81

Building a New System   83

Step One: Seed the Field   85

Getting the Word Processor under Control   86

A New Product: SyBooks — Interactive
Documentation for Sybase Products   87

Step Two: Build the Environment   88

Understanding and Supporting
Writers' Issues   89

The New System   90

The Payoffs   92

**CHAPTER 5   UNITED TECHNOLOGIES
SIKORSKY AIRCRAFT CORPORATION** **97**

Building Blocks to Better Information:
Sikorsky Aircraft Corporation   99

Twelve Weeks in the Life of
a Typical Project   100

Looking for Solutions in All
the Wrong Places   102

Fundamental Problems with the Process 103

Getting the Spin on the Right Solution 105

Selling It Upstairs 107

Picking the Solution 111

Why SGML? 112

The Fine Details: How It Works 113

Reengineering the Organization 113

Supporting the Experts with Technology . . . 115

Enhancing the Information's Value
with Attributes 117

Impact on the Organization 118

The Payoffs 119

The Electronic Products
of the Future — Today 122

    Computer-Based Training Programs 122
    Interactive Electronic Technical Manuals 122
    Expert Diagnostic Systems 123

Drawing Some Conclusions 125

CHAPTER 6   **MOBIL CORPORATION** **127**

Getting A Grip On "Gold-Plating":
Mobil Corporation 129

The Business Challenge 131

Before Technology Comes
the Problem 132

Selling the System 134

Why SGML? 135

Building EDEP, an Information-
Engineering Tool 137

EDEP in Action 139

More Than Just a Reference Book 141

Developing a Bid Document 143

How SGML Makes EDEP Possible 145

The Payoff 146

CHAPTER 7   THE SEMICONDUCTOR INDUSTRY   151

Tackling the Information Explosion at Hitachi,
Intel, National Semiconductor, Philips
Semiconductors, and Texas Instruments 153

The Business Challenge 156

The Trouble's in the Tools 158

The Beginnings of a Solution 159

Why SGML? 161

The Pinnacles Initiative:
Inventing a Revolution 162

Analyzing the Process
of Producing Information 163

Lessons from the Masters 164

The Authoring Process Turns Out
to Be a Mess 166

Turning Documents into Databases 167

The Benefits 169

CHAPTER 8   SGML INITIATIVES
IN OTHER INDUSTRIES 173

The SEC's EDGAR 176

CHAPTER 9 **LESSONS FOR YOUR FUTURE:
LEARNING FROM THE CASE STUDIES** 179

What Do the Case Studies
Have in Common? 181

All Were Championed by People
Who Could See "the Big Picture" 182

All Were Initiated by People Who
Were Experts on Their Information 184

All Looked Past the Software and Focused
on the Value of the Information Itself 186

Is This Really a Billion Dollar Secret? 188

Is SGML Right for Your Organization? 195

Do You Work with Key Documents? 196

Are You Managing Your
Information Content, or Its Publication? 198

Are You Ready to Protect the
Value of Your Information? 201

AFTERWORD: FINDING OUT MORE ABOUT SGML 205

Sources of Information on the Internet 206

Organizations Involved with SGML 207

INDEX 210

Figures

Figure 1-1   Corporate data, yesterday and today   3

Figure 1-2   Corporate documents, yesterday and today . .   5

Figure 1-3   Typical company's flow of information   8

Figure 1-4   Today's database reporting tools   12

Figure 1-5   Today's wordprocessing tools   14

Figure 1-6   Simple database   18

Figure 1-7   Text structures and formats   21

Figure 1-8   Text structures and SGML elements   25

Figure 3-1   Grolier's CD-ROM Encyclopedia   47

Figure 3-2   The editor's challenge   50

Figure 3-3   Sample editorial workflow   54

Figure 3-4   Linking related text   60

Figure 4-1   Mainframe vs. client/server computing   75

Figure 4-2   SGML filters   83

Figure 4-3   SyBook's production flow   91

Figure 4-4   SyBook's on the Web   95

Figure 5-1   Sikorsky's original workflow   101

Figure 5-2   Sikorsky's database-centered workflow   110

Figure 5-3   Reusing different text for different helicopter . .   116

Figure 5-4   Interactive Electronic Technical Manual   121

Figure 5-5   Sikorsky's Interactive Electronic
               Technical Manual 123

Figure 6-1   Mobil offshore production facility 130

Figure 6-2   EDEP system workflow 142

Figure 7-1   The ENIAC computer and the ENIAC chip . . . 154

Figure 7-2   Chips can identify your pet 155

Figure 7-3   Semiconductor data available on the Web . . . 170

Foreword

There is a black hole in most large enterprises into which money flows like a river and vital assets disappear without a trace, never to be seen again.

You know that the black hole is there. It is called "documentation" or "in-house publishing" or "support publications" or many similar things. The money goes for tasks like designing, writing, drafting, revising, searching, converting, formatting, and printing. Then it goes again for redoing these same tasks over and over as products change slightly, new markets emerge, or new forms of information delivery become available.

The vital assets that disappear are the experience, special knowledge, and collected wisdom of your employees — the information, in a word, that makes your enterprise work and be successful. It disappears because your enterprise is spending money to produce publications, rather than managing and controlling its documentary information asset.

And because you can't manage that asset:

•You can't respond quickly enough to new opportunities.

•You can't provide the service and support levels your customers demand (and deserve).

•You can't, in a word, become as **efficient** as you need to be to survive and prosper in a competitive information-based world.

This is the last untamed frontier of management: real information! Not the abstracted, orderly stuff that goes into database tables, but the information in documents of all kinds that flows through your enterprise.

Chet Ensign has been exploring this frontier for many years. And he has found many companies — including household names whose products you know and use — that have succeeded in taming it. These enterprises share a billion dollar secret: they use the Standard Generalized Markup Language (SGML) to manage their documentary information.

And they don't just shuffle around digitized images with long filenames and call it "document management." With SGML they get at the heart and soul of the information — its structure and its meaning. They get even greater control and flexibility than they have for their business transaction data.

Chet brings an expert eye to this work. He has been on the inside of companies that have had — and used SGML to solve — the communication problems that complicate the coordination of projects. He is also an internationally renowned speaker on SGML, and a founder and chairperson of the SGML Forum of New York. As chair of the External Communications Committee for SGML Open, the SGML industry consortium, he has helped bring the SGML "secret" to the world.

In this book he shares that billion dollar secret with you, in the form of engaging real-life case studies, written for the non-technical business executive. You'll learn how to manage those vital assets in your own enterprise, and how to use SGML to plug the black hole, as other smart companies have done.

And it literally is a "billion dollar secret," because SGML's cost-benefit ratio is phenomenal. Just the industries profiled in this book (and there are many, many others) have already saved over a billion dollars using SGML. Read on and Chet will show you how.

—Charles F. Goldfarb
    Saratoga, CA
    September, 1996

Introduction

*This book is not about technology . . . its real topic is a major
underexploited asset in your company; the information stored in documents.*

A BOOK FOR EXECUTIVES

If you are a member of the intended audience for this book, then you are a
business person — a senior executive, a general partner, a director or depart-
mental manager. Whatever your title or role, you work far more as a "gener-
alist" than as a "technologist." So why should you read a book that appears to
be about technology — a technology used to put books on CD-ROMs, turn
documents into databases, or publish information on the World Wide Web?

You already have plenty of books and articles to read. Not to mention
reports, email messages, and maybe even a few of those old-fashioned things
called "memos." And you have people in your company whose job is to handle technology issues. It is their responsibility to keep up with technology
developments, to recommend what products to buy, and to offer advice on
building the kinds of systems your company needs. Why should you read this
book instead of just giving it to them?

Well, you should read this book because it is *not* about technology. It dis-
cusses a technology, true — a technology known as the Standard Generalized

Markup Language, or "SGML." But its real topic is a major underexploited and uncontrolled asset in your company: the information that is created, stored, maintained, and distributed as documents. Information that ought to be as useful and as valuable to your company as the facts and statistics that you capture and store in databases, but that currently is not. This book is about why that information — that intellectual capital that your company spends money developing and that you could be leveraging for competitive advantage or putting to commercial use — is underexploited and poorly controlled despite years of investments in high-powered desktop computers and software. It is about why your technologists have not, by and large, recognized the extent of this problem and addressed it already. Most of all, it is about companies that did recognize their problem in managing this information and about how they used SGML to solve it, with tangible benefits that went far beyond their original goals.

The problems that SGML addresses can easily be costing you millions.

And this book is about what you can learn from those companies — indeed, what you must learn from them. Because your technologists can tell you how to solve problems. It is your job to tell them what problems to solve. That is why you should read this book: because it is not so much about a new technology as about a better way of thinking about your company's documents and the information they contain. It is about a fundamental business issue, and the resolution of such issues must begin with you.

WHY "THE BILLION DOLLAR SECRET"?

SGML gives your organization a degree of control over documents and the information found in them, that you never had before. But does this really make it a billion dollar secret weapon? For any one company, obviously not. Most of us would be ecstatically happy to see our companies achieve billion dollar sales, much less find billion dollar savings. But when you look at the costs of manipulating document-based information on the scale of whole industries, a billion dollars starts to look conservative. Just adding up all the direct and indirect savings achieved by companies mentioned in this book, and factoring in all the new products and capabilities SGML made possible, you can see a good start on a billion dollars.

Consider your own organization. If it is a medium- to large-sized organization, then the problems that SGML addresses can easily be costing you millions. These millions are spent:

- Finding out which of the three different answers you got from three different design engineers is correct, because you don't have a pool of design specifications and status information that all the groups involved in the product development effort share.
- Retyping or reformatting the information one department sent you before the people in your department can use it.
- Writing yet again content that has already been published, because you can't get your hands on the existing copy — and, even if you could, it would be in the wrong file format anyway.
- Redoing the files you received from one of your component suppliers before you can integrate it into your own product documentation because, even though they gave it to you in your word processor's format (an additional task for them; an additional cost for you), it is still organized completely differently from your corporate style.
- Providing phone support to customers because the information shipped with your product was incomplete.
- Handling the rejects sent back by your customer's QA department because they tested your product against your published specs, which were already out of date by the time you shipped the product out the door.

Taken individually, these problems may not be enormously costly or time consuming. It may be a hour of an engineer's time here, half a day of a technical writer's time there. It may be the three extra people you have to put on your customer-support hotline. But the problems are chronic. They are a steady friction that slows down your whole organization. They hamstring your ability to bring state-of-the-art products to market quickly. They impede internal communications, hampering your people's ability to coordinate their activities with one another. They force you to spend money recreating content you have already produced each time you want to reuse it. They detract from your company's image by making it difficult, even impossible, to deliver consistent, accurate, branded information to your customers.

These hidden — and not-so-hidden — costs are real. They are a direct result of our inability to cope with the explosion of information that our ever more technologically sophisticated economy produces. And they add up fast, once you start to look for them. They become millions of dollars in your own business very quickly. Look at them across whole industries — as thousands of companies in aviation, automobiles, semiconductors, pharmaceuticals, and other fields are doing — and the billion dollar label starts to fit.

Your organization may not experience all these problems. But it almost certainly has some of them — and others that I haven't even listed. You don't have to tolerate the lost opportunities, the diminished productivity, the poor internal coordination, and the unnecessary extra expense that traditional approaches to document-based information produce. This book tells how some very different companies in very diverse industries have attacked problems like these and solved them using SGML. Their stories have a lot to tell you about how you can identify and address the same sorts of problems and opportunities in your own business.

HOW THE BOOK IS ORGANIZED

This book is written so that you can use it to learn what you need to know quickly. Ideally, you will read all the case studies. Often companies discover that the information problem they thought they were trying to address, whether it was building a World Wide Web site to support customer service or publishing their technical product information on a CD-ROM, turns into a very different set of problems once they get started building the solution. Reading about the variety of problems that other companies have tackled can help give you a broader set of ideas for solving your own.

However, you can also read this book in bits and pieces. Each case study is a story unto itself. You can start with the cases that seem most relevant to your business or situation and read the others at your leisure. Each case study is introduced with an executive summary that provides an overview of the company's business, the problem they had, and how they solved it.

You don't have to tolerate lost opportunities, diminished productivity, poor internal coordination, and unnecessary expense that traditional approaches to document-based information produce.

I recommend that you read the first two chapters before turning to the case studies themselves, because those chapters set the stage for understanding what each company accomplished. Chapter 1 explains why the current technologies used to write and publish documents has failed to provide us with useful pools of information assets. The documents our companies create are not "data" in the way that our customer databases or our automated order-entry systems or our financial records are. This chapter explains why, and it introduces another approach to creating and managing that information that dramatically changes what we can do with it.

Chapter 2 is a fictional account of what happens when a sophisticated, technology-adept corporation attempts to use its reservoir of technical information to build a state-of-the-art product-support tool. Trying to deliver a strategic system that will greatly benefit their customers and further cement their position as a market leader, they instead get an object lesson in just how ill suited most of today's electronic documents are for anything more than printing out brochures and manuals. The story is hypothetical — but that doesn't mean it isn't true. The events it relates are drawn from years of personal experience and the experiences of others who have tried to create new information products for their companies. It is the story of what might well happen in *your* company when you try to leverage the content that you have been paying to create for all these years. The names have been changed to protect the innocent, but the story itself is very real and it is being played out in companies around the world every working day.

ACKNOWLEDGMENTS

Now that I am winding up this project, I find myself paying attention to the acknowledgments section in other books. I used to skip over them, but no more. I read them now because they mean something to me. They say that a book was not a solitary exercise but instead the outcome of a community of effort. It was the result of one person's work, perhaps, but of many people's input and ongoing support. Certainly that has been true of this book, where I have tried to capture and convey experiences and successes achieved by others. I owe much to my community, and if this book has anything useful to say, it is only because, like Newton, I have stood "upon the shoulders of giants."

First and foremost, I want to thank Dr. Charles Goldfarb for realizing that I had a book in me before I realized it myself. If Charles had not seen the seeds of this book in some of the material that I had posted to comp.text.sgml, the Internet SGML newsgroup, I would have missed this opportunity to learn firsthand how so many dynamic, inventive people use SGML in furthering their business objectives as well as to broaden my own understanding of the applications of technology in the workplace.

Special thanks are also due to Mark Taub, the senior managing editor for the Charles F. Goldfarb Series, for waiting patiently while I learned to be an author. Mark has been always available, always supportive, and ready to help me in any way he could. He let me turn this book into something close to what I originally envisioned while helping me keep an eye on the final target — publication. I don't think a writer could ask any more of his editor than that.

A book like this one demands a great deal of research and investigation. Even now, I wish there had been time to do more. But I would have accomplished much less had I not had the help of Fredrick T. (Tom) Martin of NSA, the National Security Agency. Tom has been a research partner and also a cheerleader, a sounding board, and a fan. Through the most demanding of times in his professional and personal life, he stayed involved in the project, tracking down leads, lining up case study candidates, and collecting information. He is one of the giants who has supported me during this project, and I cannot thank him enough.

This is primarily a book of case studies, which I could not have written without the generosity of many people. Those whose success stories are told in this book, and more whose success stories are not, gave me far more of their time, their memories, and their resources than I asked for. My deepest thanks go out to them all: Terry Badger, Jeff Barton, Elaine Brennan, Cyndie Cooper, Ed Covennan, Bert Daron, Alfred Elkerbout, Dr. Robert J. Glushko, Steve Goodman, Tom Jeffery, Ted Kell, Ken Kirschner, Vane Lashua, Debbie Lapeyre, Larry Lorimer, Pat O'Sullivan, Dave Rattanni, Joe Salerno, Gary Sargent, Paul Simpson, Lamont Thomas, Tommie Usdin, Richard Weich, and Bob Yencha.

I owe a special thank you to my employers, Darren Bryden and Mimi Brooks of Logical Design Solutions, Inc. They tolerated my absences, sudden disappearances, long phone calls, and frequent spells of distraction with quiet good humor. Without their support, this book would be far less than it is.

Many people shared ideas, reactions, insights, critiques, and a million useful observations on what worked and what didn't — in this book as well as in the real world. In particular, I am grateful to Jon Bosak, Tom Comerford, Kurt Conrad, Joseph Gangemi, Mary Laplante, and David Silverman. They helped turn my fledgling notions into concrete substance.

This book required a lot of travel. That's what advances are for, of course, but the credit card companies would have been gleefully raising my credit limit even higher had it not been for Natalie Burgio at The Travel Gallery in Madison, NJ. Natalie took sympathy on my situation and made it her personal mission to get me to and from my various destinations at the lowest possible expense. Thanks Natalie — the book is done and I won't have to file for bankruptcy afterall.

To Karen Florman and Francis Gambino I'll just say, "Thanks for telling me that I could do this." How many times?

Finally, no amount of thanks can come close to repaying my wife Barbara and my daughter Emma for their support, encouragement, patience, and love throughout this project. Especially the patience part. A book is like a second full-time job, and there were many sunny weekends and family events when they went off and left me behind closed doors, working on "the dumb book." Through all of it, they put up with me with grace and (for the most part) good humor. I love you both — now we can go back to living the life to which we were accustomed.

—Chet Ensign

CHAPTER 1

The Cottage Industry Right Under Your Nose

Investments in PCs, GUI operating systems and WYSIWYG word processors have only improved your ability to generate paper, not information.

If your company is like most, you have made a significant investment in computer infrastructures over the last ten years or so. Your company has purchased personal computers, UNIX workstations, high-speed printers, networks, and more. Much of that investment has been committed to hardware and software used for creating documents. Virtually 100% of today's business computer users have word processing programs; many use their computers almost exclusively for writing. Also, if your company is like most, you have not — despite these investments — dramatically improved your ability to produce or use that information efficiently.

To produce *paper*, yes. Your paper budget is almost certainly growing every year. The advent of personal computers and high-quality laser printers has drastically cut the cost and effort needed to create documents that once required the services of a professional typesetter. Overall commercial shipments of the uncoated sheet paper used by laser printers and copiers are predicted to go up 6% annually through the rest of the decade, according to the *American Forest and Paper Association*. The *Business and Institutional Furniture Manufacturers' Association* reports that sales of file cabinets grew by 29%

between 1991 and 1994 and are expected to continue growing in the years ahead.

Paper, yes. But information? Not necessarily.

You are certainly creating more documents. Yours is the rare corporate entity if it is not. You are probably producing more of the documents that you have always produced: legal and financial documents, reports and surveys, catalogs, brochures and other marketing collateral, engineering designs and technical specifications, owner's manuals, not to mention a host of required government filings.

You are also likely to be producing new types of documents as well — information in forms that you never produced before: custom manuals created for individual clients, computerized training programs for your employees on CD-ROMs, policy and standards manuals made available over the corporate network, or marketing materials on the World Wide Web. New channels and uses for information seem to pop up every day.

The costs are significant, but difficult to measure: lost employee effectiveness, missed market opportunities, increased customer support costs and decreased customer satisfaction.

For your fact-based data — financial records, inventory levels, plant performance, and the like — you have probably had significant productivity improvements. The software programs called databases have substantially improved your organization's ability to collect, track, analyze, and distribute that information in a timely manner. The archetypal picture of a cavernous office filled with endless rows of desks where clerks labor away at the company's books is a thing of the past. In many companies today, managers and executives expect to be no more than a push button away from up-to-the-minute reports on financial performance and industry indicators (see Figure 1–1).

Important as fact-based data is, it is not the only type of information a company requires. Your company also runs on — and depends for its growth and survival on — the richer and far more complex types of information carried in documents. According to Frank Gilbane, Editorial Director of *The Gilbane Report on Open Information and Document Systems*, "fact-based, statistical data represents only around 20% of the information in your company. The other 80% is in documents."

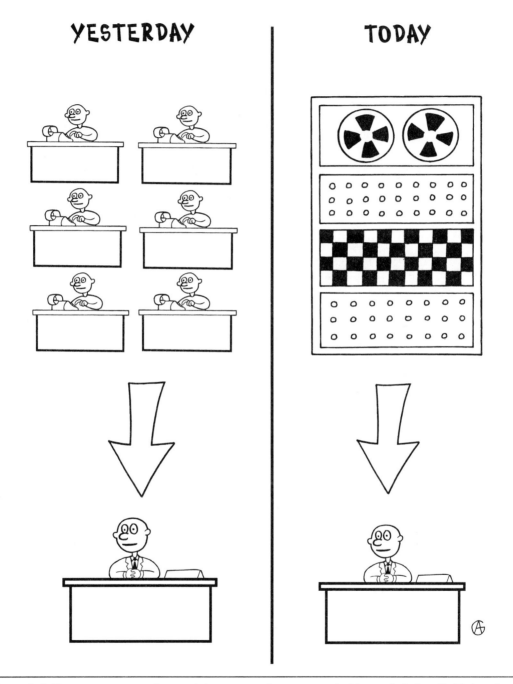

Figure 1–1. To report on operating statistics, companies once needed large clerical staffs. Today, those tasks are automated.

That 80% encompasses various categories of documents. Many of those documents carry information that is crucial to your company's success. It is information that transfers knowledge and enables people to make informed decisions and take intelligent action. You can, for example, "empower" your employees by giving them direct access to sales, pricing, and inventory databases, but if they don't have simultaneous access to the policies and guidelines to guide their decision making, access to the numbers will result in no meaningful action — or worse, the wrong action.

Documents are the vehicle for a wide variety of information flows crucial to supporting and achieving corporate goals. *And this is where the investments in computer technology have shown little return.* Because in most companies today, the investments in PCs, GUI operating systems, and WYSIWYG word processors have only improved your ability to generate paper, *not* information. The costs associated with creating, managing, and using all that paper rise in lockstep with its volume. For every additional document you want to — or have to — produce, it seems you always need another analyst, another writer, another desktop publisher or designer, and newer software. Picture that cavernous office filled with endless rows of desks where writers labor away at company documents (see Figure 1–2). That picture has not changed.

In recent years, movements focused on improving corporate effectiveness have become virtual household names: Total Quality Management (TQM), ISO 9000, Reengineering, and so on. Their popularity and persistence — if not always their success — are evidence of widespread recognition by corporate management that companies need to do a better job of coordinating activities across the entire enterprise. Managers have recognized that the inability to control internal processes bogs their companies down and prevents them from meeting critical goals, such as:

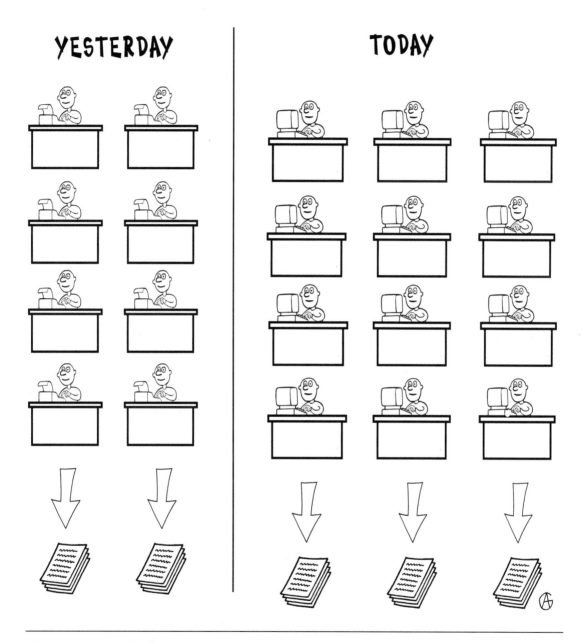

Figure 1–2. To publish information, companies once needed large staffs of authors and typists. Today, most need even more.

- Responding quickly to new market opportunities
- Providing better service and support to their customers
- Improving staff efficiency
- Reducing costs while delivering better service

Solving these problems has become a mantra of corporate survival, as well as a major focus of technology development. The one area that hasn't been recognized as demanding the same degree of high-level, enterprisewide attention is document-type information processing — looking for ways to manage the information instead of the piece of paper. The costs to your company are significant, if difficult to measure with precision: lost employee effectiveness, missed market opportunities, increased customer support costs and decreased customer satisfaction.

Think of this as the next frontier of modern business management. The pioneers have been there already. The case studies in this book present just a few of their stories. These firms revisited the basic notion of the "document" and adopted an approach that distinguishes the information they create from the forms in which it is delivered. They developed tools and techniques to change their growing masses of documents into rich information assets that can be as efficiently manipulated by computers for mechanical, production types of tasks as they can by humans for creative and analytical types of tasks. They have done this by taking advantage of the international standard known as the *Standard Generalized Markup Language*, more commonly referred to as *SGML*.

DOCUMENT-BASED INFORMATION IS CRUCIAL TO YOUR COMPANY

You may be tempted to think of documents as "lightweight" resources, not "real" information like that in your financial, manufacturing, and inventory databases. Certainly there are significant differences between the two. However, lest you be tempted to dismiss documents as unimportant, let's look at the role they play in the life of a company.

If information is the life blood of a company, documents are its red blood cells. They are the carriers of a vital flow of information. Your company may be a traditional manufacturer, or it may be a new-age consulting firm. You may make semiconductors or industrial chemicals or tractors. You may deliver long-distance phone service or you may deliver packages. You may program software. You may program people. No matter what you make or do, the people inside your company engage in a variety of activities in order to make your products, and the people outside your company engage in a variety of activities in order to use them. All of these activities run on information, and most of it is delivered via documents (see Figure 1–3).

Internally, documents are crucial to your daily operations. They set up and maintain the "rules of the game" that allow all the different teams to work together. Various groups within your company depend on the information in documents to carry out a number of crucial tasks, including:

If information is the life blood of a company, documents are its red blood cells.

- Establishing and communicating "Here's how you work with us" policies and procedures
- Coordinating plans, schedules, and activities
- Defining priorities
- Setting and revising standards and specifications
- Requesting and delivering services

And, of course, they depend on documents to inform each other of changes to all of the above.

Picture the manufacturing department trying to tool up for a new product without knowing about engineering's design changes. Picture engineering trying to modify the product without knowing the types of problems manufacturing has encountered. Picture sales trying to sell the product without knowing whether manufacturing can deliver

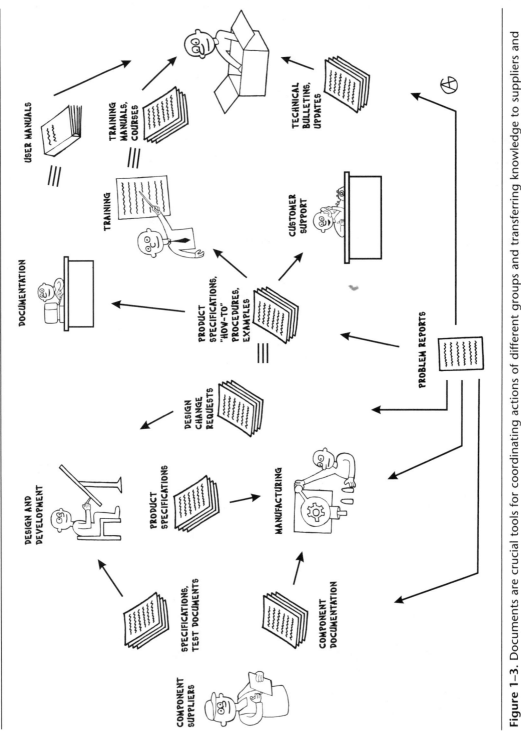

Figure 1–3. Documents are crucial tools for coordinating actions of different groups and transferring knowledge to suppliers and customers.

it. Picture customer service trying to answer a customer's questions without knowing how the product works. No one in your organization works in a void; every group has to be able to communicate with others in order to function effectively. Documents are the vehicles they use for that communication.

Externally, documents are vital to finding customers and keeping them. They are your primary — and certainly your most cost-effective — means for telling potential customers that your product exists, why they should buy it, how to buy it, and how to use it effectively and safely once they have it in their hands. The personal touch is an important part of your success. But no sizable company can afford to conduct all its business face-to-face. Your company relies on documents to:

- Notify potential customers of your product's existence
- Notify existing customers of new developments
- Position your product in the marketplace and tell people why they should buy it
- Supply legally required information to customers, partners, and regulators
- Execute purchases and communicate specifications and customizations back to the company
- Explain how to use your products
- Let customers know how to contact your company for help and suggestions

Almost every internal and external process has its accompanying document. Every hire, every fire, every goal, every mission, every engineering design, every manufacturing change, every quality test, every technical review, every request for services . . . everything that gets anything done in your company is started by or results in a document. And if your company has seriously entertained any of those initiatives to improve the way you do business (TQM, Reengineering, and so on), then you have added even more documents to the number you were already producing. Each of those standards relies on thorough documentation of processes inside your organization.

Information is one of the most critical resources your company possesses. The intellectual property that your company grows and develops is what distinguishes you from your competition. Without information — not just the relatively simple, fact-type data stored in databases, but also the richer, more action-oriented information conveyed by documents — there can be no sharing or exchanging of knowledge. And without that base of knowledge, your employees can't engage in the kinds of intelligent behaviors that will make your company successful.

Given their pivotal role as carriers of critical information, why aren't we getting more productivity out of our investments in document-producing systems? Where's the reuse of the material once it is written? Where's the leveraging of existing content for new documents or distribution media? Why aren't we becoming more efficient at creating and using this information?

In a word: why are we treating this vital resource as an expense item when we should be managing it as an asset?

THE PRODUCTIVITY DILEMMA WITH DOCUMENTS

The reason we have not become more productive at exploiting the information in documents can be found in the tools we use to create them and the fundamental notions that those tools are based on.

When we look back at how the computer affected our ability to collect and manage fact-based data, we find that it did more than just speed up the existing methods for keeping records. It revolutionized the way we think about those records.

The first generations of computer programs defined, collected, and stored their data completely independently of other programs. Each program would define its own data format, and these were generally different from the formats being used by other programs. Information that one program collected was not available to any other program that might have a use for it. Social Security numbers, part numbers, prices, etc. were separately collected and stored by each program that needed to use them.

Then, in the 1970s, computer scientists rethought the fundamental questions of data. They rewrote the book on what it is, how we get it, how we store it, and how we manipulate it once it is there. The key concept in this revolution was the notion that data could be stored and described in a standard way, independent of the programs that created and used it. Information could be stored in one central location — a database — and made available to any program that needed to use it (see Figure 1–4).

An entirely new generation of tools developed as a result, and the whole chain of processing for fact-based data changed: ATM machines and bar-code scanners now supplement keyboards and cash registers as tools for collecting the data; networks instantaneously carry records of transactions to central databases; reporting and analysis software programs watch the trends in those databases and can report on them at a moment's notice. The whole process of creating the data, storing the data, and using the data has been not just automated but transformed by the advent of the computer.

We are still waiting for the same thing to happen to documents.

The process of creating, storing, and using document-based information has *not* been transformed by the computer. While the hardware and the software we use to create documents have dramatically improved over the years, they haven't changed the fundamental "words-on-paper" model popularized by Gutenberg 500 years ago.

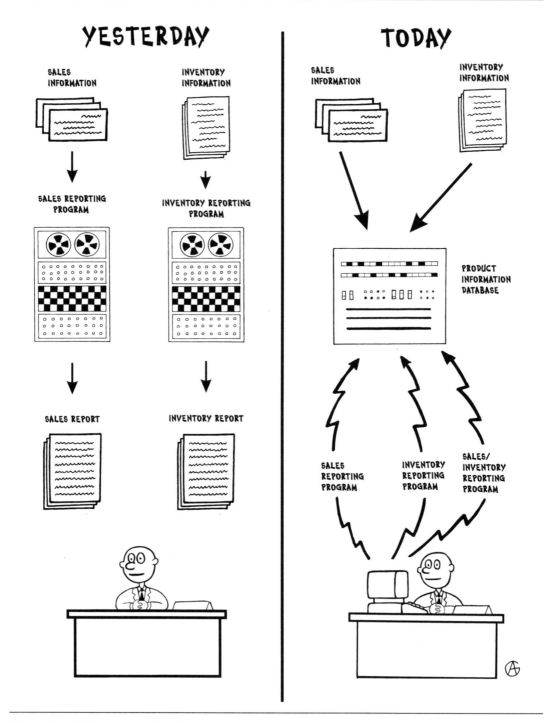

Figure 1–4. Today's generation of reporting tools transformed the way fact-based data is processed.

They are simply faster versions of the printing press. Today's word processors and desktop publishing programs give us faster and faster ways to put words on paper. But like those first generations of computer programs, they do it by storing their data — the information content that we want to distribute — in the program's own data format. Once we have printed out that final document, we've done about all with the file that we can do (see Figure 1–5).

Why? Because the files produced by your program are incompatible with the files used by mine. Think about this for a moment. If you are going to a family reunion, and you've all talked on the phone and decided to pool everyone's videotapes in order to make a documentary of the gathering, do you all have to use the same make and model of video camera? Of course not. Everybody uses the VCR he prefers. After the party, you can bring all the tapes together for editing, because all the VCRs record the video the same way. The cameras can even use different physical media — VHS, VHS-C, or Video 8. The images can still be combined because they all use the same *logical* data format.

You cannot give that same freedom of choice to the people who produce documents in your company. Regardless of need or personal preference, regardless of whether the authoring system that is right for engineering is overkill for the marketing department or vice versa, you cannot allow individuals or groups to use their tool of choice if you want them to be able to exchange documents, because the tools don't "record the text" the same way. The files they produce are incompatible.

The result of this incompatibility is that information initially created in a document is not immediately open to use by other programs for other purposes, such as analyzing it, delivering it over newswires, making it part of an interactive expert system, or publishing it on the World Wide Web. Repair procedures, financial analyses, field reports, etc. are still separately created and stored by each program that needs to use them in a document. If the content of one document could be useful in another, it must be found, copied, and often completely retyped or reformatted — a laborious and expensive manual process.

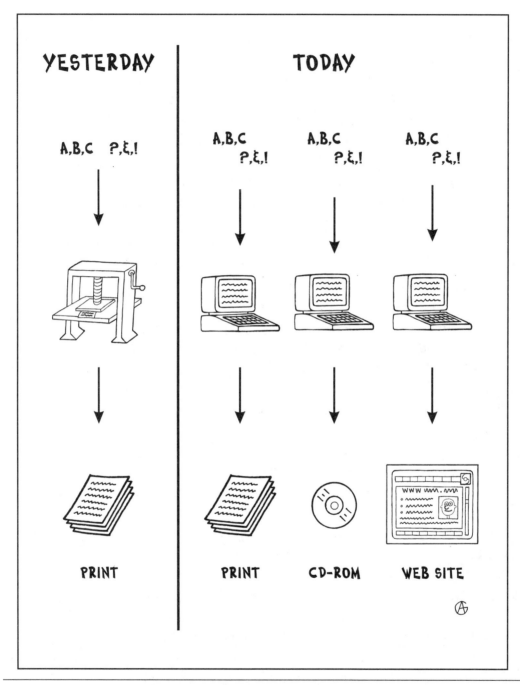

Figure 1–5. Today's generation of word processing tools has not transformed the way documents are processed.

Unlike corporate databases, documents continue to be produced, managed, and delivered in a very ad hoc fashion, usually in response to a demand for one particular end product: a user manual, a help system, a Web page. Little or no thought is given to the use of that content above and beyond the immediate objective. Once you begin to see this at work in your organization, you begin to see its negative impact on productivity — and its positive impact on your company's underlying costs.

WRITING DOCUMENT-BASED INFORMATION: THE NEW COTTAGE INDUSTRY

Writing remains a virtual cottage industry. Remember cottage industries? A merchant would come to a village and pass out wool. The villagers would take the wool home, knit up as many sweaters as they could, and bring them back to the merchant when they were done.

Well, move that model into every part of your company where documents get created. That's still how it's done today. We don't go to a village, of course. We go to market research, technical documentation, or legal. And the raw material is no longer wool. It is facts, statistics, specifications, requirements, regulations, or instructions. But your skilled, creative, professional people still take that information and go back to their offices where they sit down at PCs so powerful that they could have run the air traffic control system in the '60s, and they knit sweaters.

Well, O.K. They don't knit sweaters. They write documents. But those documents, like those hand-knit sweaters, are one-off items, custom-crafted works of art. Aside from printing them on paper (either paper paper or some electronic equivalent of paper), there is not much the computer can do with them. Computers are far faster and more accurate than people; nevertheless, you can't use the computer to rebuild those documents into new products and forms. If you want to leverage content that someone has already created, you have to get a human being involved.

For example:

- Do you want to extract explanations and procedures from a user manual and reuse them for customer-training textbooks? Nothing stored in the word processor file can let a computer distinguish which parts of the document should be used for theory and training and extract them for you. A human being is going to have to do the work. A person will have to go through the manual and find the relevant pieces, copy them out, and put them into the textbook's format.

- Do you want to distribute your press releases and your annual report over several online services as well as your World Wide Web homepage? Good luck. Every one of those distribution channels — newswire, online database, and World Wide Web — requires that the information be formatted and organized differently, and none of the formats matches what your word processor produces. So get a human being or two. They'll disassemble the text and the graphics from your desktop publishing package and reformat them for each of those delivery systems.

- Do you want to offer your customers an expert diagnostic system, applying your existing documentation to help them use your product effectively and quickly troubleshoot problems? There are no markers in the document's source files that will let a computer automatically link the diagnostic system to the documentation. Budget a few hundred thousand dollars and collect a small army of people, because you are going to have to rebuild the documentation from scratch in order to use it in this new system.

It shouldn't be this way. It doesn't have to be this way. A computer *could* be doing most or all of the production work for you, many orders of magnitude faster than any person could. A computer could be doing the chores, freeing your staff to focus on creative work that really adds value for your customers. Computers are good at mechanical, predictable tasks. Human beings are good at being creative. But computers cannot do that kind of mechanical work on documents, because the documents produced by today's high-powered, WYSIWYG tools don't represent the kind of general-purpose data that can be used for a variety of applications.

COMPUTERS CAN PERFORM MIRACLES — <u>WHEN</u> THEY HAVE THE RIGHT DATA

In their book *README.1ST: SGML for Writers and Editors*, Ron Turner, Timothy Douglass, and Audrey Turner describe the goal of developing "documents that are totally open — rendered in ways unknown to the author and only later defined, shareable across all computing architectures, portable among an entire community, reusable in ways also as yet undefined."[1] They contrast that with today's reality of documents that are "locked in to a particular computer, operating system, network, or page layout program." Our investments in desktop computing could be giving us information that meets the goal — *if* they had the right data to work with.

Let's brush aside the razzle-dazzle of the computer ads for a moment and get back to common-sense basics. Computers are what you always thought they were — dumb boxes. Clever collections of switches. They don't have any real intelligence at all.

But they are blindingly fast and precise. They can execute millions of operations in the time that it takes you or me to remember where to put our finger in order to type the "Q" key. Computers can be tremendously versatile and extremely productive — if they have a predictable input to execute those instructions upon. Let's call that input "data."

The word "data" is used here to mean information that has a consistent, predictable, and meaningful structure. To qualify as "data," the same pieces of information must be identified the same way each time the computer encounters them. Project numbers are always marked this

Computers could be doing production work orders of magnitude faster than a person. But they can't because the documents produced by today's high-powered, WYSIWYG tools aren't general-purpose data.

---

1 Ron Turner, Timothy Douglass, and Audrey Turner, *README.1ST: SGML for Writers and Editors*, Upper Saddle River, NJ: Prentice Hall, 1996.

way; retail prices are always flagged that way. You will know that this is a procedure and not another kind of numbered list because it will be precisely identified as such. Computers are not nearly as good at working with the unpredictable as we are. But tell a computer exactly what to expect and exactly what to do with it when it finds it, and you get the miracles large and small that we see around us every day.

Databases work as well as they do because the fact-based data stored in them is divided into well-defined categories, generally referred to as "fields" (see Figure 1–6). The computer knows that information found in a particular field represents a specific kind of fact — the volume of a package, for example, or the status code for a project, or the dollar amount of a transaction. Because the computer can be told how to identify the different types of data, programs can be written to analyze the data: tabulate it, graph it, react to it if it goes outside predefined norms, and so on.

Product Number	Description	Inventory	Unit Cost
A001	Capital A, Times Roman	125	0.02
A002	Capital A, Helvetica	83	0.02
A003	Lower case A, Times Roman	274	0.02
A004	Lower case A, Helvetica	821	0.01
B001	Capital B, Times Roman	97	0.03
B002	Capital B, Helvetica	96	0.03

Figure 1–6. Factual data can be stored in well-defined, consistent categories.

This isn't such a foreign concept. It is really just another type of raw material. What do you typically try to do with raw materials? You try to standardize them as much as possible so that you can maximize your internal efficiency. This, after all, is what standards are all about. Can you picture an automobile industry if ball bearings, gaskets, and spark plugs weren't made in standard sizes? If you could burn only GM gasoline in your GM car? Would there be video rental stores and huge music stores if every movie and music studio used its own recording medium and format? For that matter, in the United States it wasn't all that long ago that the ultimate raw material — money — was still being freely issued by banks and states. What would the U.S. economy be like today if it had not established a central currency?

Data is a computer's raw material. Knowing the structure and meaning of the data, and knowing the output you want to produce, you can exploit the speed and accuracy of the computer to produce the output.

TODAY'S "DOCUMENTS" ARE NOT "DATA"

The documents produced by most of the word processors and desktop publishing programs used in your company are not data — not in the sense of the word used here. They represent a very limited-use type of data, good for creating one finished product, which is usually attractive sheets of paper. But to republish or change that output to something else, such as a CD-ROM, you cannot simply switch to a different program and reuse the data. You have to go back and change the information itself.

Why? Because the two most important characteristics of data — predictability and meaningful structure — are not part of today's ordinary word processing and desktop publishing programs.

While today's WYSIWYG writing tools produce predictably formatted printed pages, the files they create to store them are highly *un*predictable. Every program on the market gives its users several different ways to create any given visual effect on the page. Typefaces and sizes, bolding and italics, indents and rules can all be done multiple ways. The more powerful the program, the more ways there are to create visual effects. The result is that the appearance of the printed page tells you nothing about the data inside the file that created it. Two printed pages can look identical, yet the files that produce them can be completely different.

The tools also place no constraints on the visual effects that a writer can choose to create. WYSIWYG programs let writers produce any WYSIWYG they want. Your company may have a published style guide that specifies how documents should be formatted and information presented, but compliance with that style guide is strictly on the honor system. If a writer chooses to use a different font for the body copy, or indent lists differently, or use bold instead of italics, there's nothing in the program to prevent it from happening. In practice, most documents within an organization have differences in their formatting, sometimes minor, but sometimes surprisingly large.

In fact, when several different writers have worked on a document over a period of time, it is common to find the same types of content — lists, tables, examples — done in different ways. This is what makes it so difficult to reprocess these files for new and different purposes. In order to write a program that can use a WYSIWYG document as its raw material, the programmer has to anticipate every variation on formatting that writers could produce and write a procedure to manipulate it. In practice, writers can come up with unanticipated ways to format text far faster than programmers can write computer programs to process them.

The second characteristic of data — meaningful structure — is also notably lacking in today's WYSIWYG programs. It is the structure that provides meaning about the data. It is what turns *data* into *information*. For example, it is how we know that an occurrence of the number "5" in a database tells us how many boxes of finishing nails we have in stock instead of how much they cost.

Unlike databases, where data is structured consistently, WYSIWYG programs have traditionally added only enough structure to their data to control how the final printout looks (see Figure 1–7). For example, your company's documents might print citations, emphasized words and phrases, cautions and warnings in italics. But the files do not structure that text in ways that let us — or our computers — distinguish the citations from the warnings, etc. The files store instructions to "make this text italic." What if tomorrow your legal department recommends that warnings be printed in red ink instead? You will not be able to make that change by tweaking the program that prints the files, because there is no completely dependable way for a computer program to distinguish the warnings from other italicized text. People will have to read through all your documents and make the change by hand. (One indicator of the growing recognition of the limitations of this model: many of the successful WYSIWYG word processing and desktop publishing software manufacturers have introduced SGML-aware versions of their products over the past few years.)

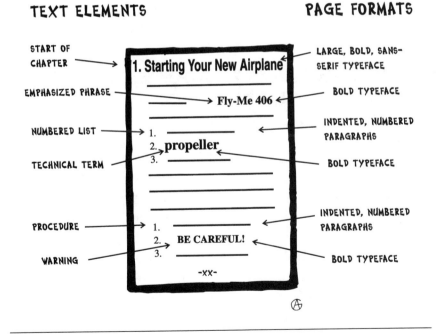

Figure 1–7. The commands that format text give us no information about its significance to the document.

WYSIWYG tools have had tremendous success in the market because, in addition to being relatively inexpensive, they have made authors, personally speaking, very productive. Reports that once required a writer, a paste-up artist, and a typesetter can now be done by one person using a good desktop publishing program. But personal productivity sometimes comes at the expense of the productivity of the organization. The impact of these output-oriented writing tools on the bottom line has been anything but marginal. The ability of our organizations to economically create and exploit information in documents has been significantly compromised by these "personal productivity" tools.

If there were some way to turn documents into information resources, carriers of predictable and meaningfully structured data that could be shared and exploited by a variety of different programs to produce a variety of different outputs, we could begin to realize the productivity payoffs from documents that we have already seen from databases. And there is one way to do it.

FROM DOCUMENTS TO INFORMATION: ENTER SGML, THE STANDARD GENERALIZED MARKUP LANGUAGE

All documents, whether print, hypertext, or multimedia, have structures that are meaningful for their readers. In English-language books, for example, they have organizing structures like chapters and sections. They have navigating structures like the table of contents, the index, or hypertext links. They have structures that contain information like paragraphs, lists, procedures, and tables. In other languages and cultures, the structures may be different. But structures are there nonetheless. These structures are indicated to the reader by the visual clues that we call "format."

We have been reading for so long that we've become attuned to those visual clues. We use them to figure out the meanings associated with the different structures subconsciously. So it comes as no surprise that our first generation of word processing programs were tools that create format. That's what we thought the point was.

But the WYSIWYG — What You See Is What You Get — of format-controlling word processing programs might just as well be spelled WYSIAYEG — What You See Is *ALL* You'll *EVER* Get. As we have seen, controlling the format doesn't produce reusable data.

What we need is a way to structure our document-based data with meaning that goes beyond mere typography — so that we can continue to produce paper, but also use the information (the data plus its structure) for other forms of communication as well — CD-ROMs, online services, interactive programs, and more. We need a way to distinguish the content from the way it is presented.

The implications of this idea were recognized as early as 1969 by three researchers at IBM: Charles F. Goldfarb, Ed Mosher, and Raymond Lorie. They were seeking ways to share documents among different mainframe-based computer programs. The result of their efforts was the Generalized Markup Language (GML).

WYSIWYG — What You See Is What You Get — might as well be WYSIAYEG — What You See Is ALL You'll EVER Get.

In the design of GML, Goldfarb, Mosher, and Lorie took a fundamentally different approach to the information content of documents. Instead of *implying* the structure of a document by filling it with markup codes that described formatting, they chose instead to store the structures in the document explicitly. Chapters, paragraphs, lists, tables — all were identified by name instead of appearance. The mechanism they used was the inclusion of simple markup "tags" — like **:h2.**, **:p.**, or **:li.** — to identify the structure associated with the text. The tag **:h2.**, for example, identified a section title, or "heading." **:li.** identified an item in a list.

Once the structure of the document was known, computer programs could replace manual labor as the primary method of processing the information for its intended use. For example, footnotes in a printed book could be put at the bottom of a page, while in the electronic version of the book they could be displayed in a pop-up window on screen. Warnings could be changed from italic to bold red simply by changing the programs that processed the files. With GML, the information in a document was no longer welded to the program that created it. As long as a computer program was designed to be able to interpret GML, it could make use of the information in the files.

GML was adopted by IBM as the standard for its own publishing. Today, there are over 11 million pages published by IBM from GML. (Only the Federal Government prints more.) Goldfarb continued to enhance GML, inventing what would become SGML, the Standard Generalized Markup Language, in 1980. SGML was further developed by the ISO (the International Organization for Standardization) from 1980 to 1986, culminating in a formal standard, ISO 8879:1986.

Although these examples of GML tags are based on the model of a book — chapters, sections, and so on — GML's inventors realized that there could be other models of document types that different groups would want to use for their information. So GML was not designed as a predefined set of tags at all. Instead, it was designed to give the content owner a tool to develop markup languages tailored precisely to his own information. The mechanism for developing these languages was the *document type definition*, or *DTD*. In GML, a DTD was for human use only. One of the improvements in SGML is that DTDs can also be read and used by the computer.

Speaking informally, a document type definition is a set of rules that govern how SGML is applied to a particular category of documents. It describes the structure and meaning of the information components, or *elements*, that can be used in the documents, and it defines their relationships to one another. The DTD formally defines what Turner, Douglass, and Turner call, "the structural building blocks of a document."[2]

It is the DTD that lets a pharmaceutical company define solubility, optical rotation, and thermal behavior as elements in the Chemistry, Manufacturing and Controls Section of a New Drug Application

---

2 *README.1ST; SGML for Writers and Editors*, Page 55

(NDA). It is the DTD that lets a financial organization distinguish current and accrued liabilities, capital lease obligations, and long-term notes payable as distinct information components in a 10K filed with the SEC. It is the DTD that lets a software company tag executable examples differently from nonexecutable examples in a training manual. The key benefit of the DTD is that it allows the software to customize the SGML environment to describe *your* information (see Figure 1–8).

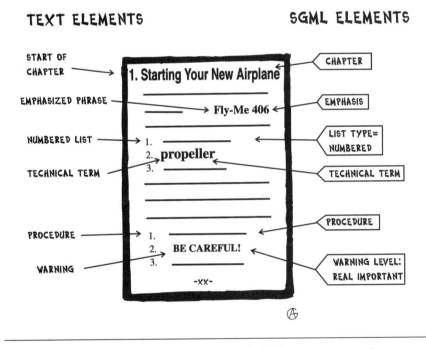

Figure 1–8. SGML structures identify text precisely. Computer processing can produce different output formats automatically.

Frank Gilbane observes that companies have begun to realize that whether they intend it to happen or not, documents are being created, stored, and delivered in electronic form. This is giving documents renewed attention in the business setting. "We are heading toward a situation where information management technology will be document centered, not data centered," he says. "We've solved the data problem. Now we have to solve the document problem."

SGML is a key piece of that solution. It has brought the same kind of predictability and general-purpose structure to document-based information that fact-based data has enjoyed for so long. The case studies in the remainder of this book give practical examples of the business benefits that result. But before we start examining them, let's look at what typically happens to a company when it first tries — without SGML — to use the information in WYSIWYG documents to solve a pressing business problem.

Building Cutting-Edge Information Products from Documents — Why It Doesn't Work Today

TypiComp, Inc. is a fiction. But its story is repeated in companies all over the world, day after day.

The stories that you will read in the later chapters of this book are success stories. They highlight companies that have found better ways to manage and exploit the information carried in documents. But they don't represent the majority of companies today. Most companies are still handling document-based information using methods that do little more than speed up the printing press.

So before we turn to those success stories, let's look at a more typical tale. Let's spend some time with a fictional company that is trying to develop an innovative new feature for its product and see what often happens when a company tries to take advantage of the information collected in its documentation.

We'll call this company TypiComp, Inc. TypiComp will be a manufacturer of test equipment for personal computers — in other words, a high-tech company with expertise in both hardware and software, a leader in a very competitive, very lucrative industry niche. Just the sort of company that you would expect could quickly develop sophisticated information packages to help its customers better use its products.

TypiComp, Inc. — its personnel, its experiences, and the problems it encounters — is a fiction. Any resemblance to real persons or companies living or dead is unintentional. However, any resemblance to the way things might work in *your* company today is absolutely intentional. Because the TypiComp story is created from real experiences, episodes, and anecdotes gathered over years of working on similar projects — some successful, some not. TypiComp is a fiction, but its story is true. The details are repeated in companies all over the world, day after day.

TAKING ON A BUSINESS CHALLENGE

TypiComp achieved early success by responding to customer needs. In the first days of the computer business, designing and delivering diagnostic equipment — "testbeds" in TypiComp lingo — was still a process that two or three engineers could manage. TypiComp, Inc. could design and deliver customized testbeds to a customer faster than anyone *and* their equipment was reliable. To a PC maker running a multimillion dollar assembly plant with a backlog of orders to fill, that kind of service and reliability was worth a premium.

But now, TypiComp is struggling to survive the fruits of its own success. Over the last few years personal computers have become orders of magnitude more powerful and complex. TypiComp's testbeds have likewise become more complicated to design and build, requiring teams not of two or three engineers but of twenty or thirty. Internal communication problems have followed.

- Engineering's lead time for designing today's increasingly specialized testbeds has stretched from weeks to months, and PC makers are demanding a return to the tight timeframes they had come to expect.

- Manufacturing is struggling to maintain its record for reliability even as products become more customized and more intricate, and the interdependencies between parts of the manufacturing process multiply.
- Training and customer service are swamped by the very information that they are charged with transmitting to TypiComp's clients, both internal and external.

And everyone is struggling to cope with the torrent of important document-based information that is central to doing their job. Technical manuals have swelled to thousands of pages; engineers spend more and more of their time writing, reviewing, and coordinating TCI's (Testbed Change Instructions) with manufacturing; customer-service personnel must now read hundreds of pages of tech bulletins each week if they want to keep up with product developments.

In order to address these problems, TypiComp's senior management decided to build the "Testbed Information Management System," affectionately known as TIMS. TIMS would become an enterprisewide system for managing this river of information, and the key to making it work was getting document-based information off paper and online.

ELECTRONIC DOCUMENTS — THE PUBLISHING PANACEA?

To TypiComp's management, the decision to put their information online looked like a no-brainer. The problem, after all, was that they simply had too much content to cope with. Sam Gelding, TypiComp's president, compared it to other information-intensive problems: "Nobody *reads* our inventory records or accounts receivable. If they need to know something, they look the numbers up in a database! All this engineering stuff ought to be handled the same way."

Sam envisioned TIMS as the vehicle for managing all the technical and engineering information, from design through manufacturing and right out to the customer, by making documentation and troubleshooting guides part of the system itself. When test engineers at customer sites had questions or problems with the equipment, they would no longer have to turn to a bookshelf full of manuals for help. They would bring the information up on a screen right there on the machine. TypiComp management began to envision a day, not too far off, when TypiComp testbeds could run self-diagnosing software tied directly into the installed documentation. The testbeds would automatically identify problems, display suggested courses of action for the users, even dial up TypiComp customer support to retrieve any new and relevant technical bulletins, and email a customer support rep a description of the problem.

The benefits to TypiComp would be significant: faster product development; fewer customer service calls; reduced printing costs; more satisfied customers.

The benefits to TypiComp would be significant: better internal coordination leading to faster product development; fewer calls to customer service; reduced cost of printing and storing manuals; more satisfied customers.

Idealistic? Naive? Blue sky? Not at all. Initiatives like TIMS are under development in every industry with complex products, from Silicon Valley, to the Motor City, to Wall Street. (In fact, for some real-world examples of similar undertakings, read the case studies on Sikorsky Aircraft and the semiconductor industry's Pinnacles Initiative.) TypiComp's senior executives, like those in many other industries, simply recognized an information-management problem in their business and took assertive steps to remedy it.

But take note: central to this undertaking is the concept that there is "information" in TypiComp's documents that can be managed and manipulated by a computer. TypiComp was about to get the same rude awakening that others have gotten; no one had yet looked into what it would take to turn their printed manuals into usable electronic information.

THE LESSONS OF THE PROTOTYPE

TypiComp was not a company you could criticize for being "penny wise and pound foolish." Over the years, as the company invested in computer-aided-design (CAD) systems for building its products, it also invested in writing and desktop publishing software for producing supporting information. Engineers and technical writers all worked on high-powered workstations with state-of-the-art WYSIWYG word processors. Everyone was connected to the corporate network and email system. In fact, management was frustrated with the communication difficulties of recent years precisely *because* so much money had been invested in word processing tools. "We've spent a fortune buying people those word processors they wanted!" Sam exclaimed. "So why can't they process those words more productively?!"

Because these investments had been made over time, management now expected to see a payback in the form of rapid implementation of TIMS. And, in fact, early initiatives looked very promising. A team was assembled under Margaret Lemming, TypiComp's chief information officer, to build a TIMS prototype. Using sample files from the technical writing department and TCIs from engineering, they built a TIMS prototype in just one month, using off-the-shelf technology. "It looked great!" Margaret remembers. "So great that we gave it big play at the next board meeting — mainly to get the board off our backs." Expectations ran high.

To be sure, there were some clues to what lay ahead. An important part of TIMS was the linking of related information with hypertext links. In a hypertext system, the reader can click on a highlighted piece of text, such as a "For more information, see . . ." cross reference, and immediately "jump to" the referenced information. Hypertext linking was doubly important to TIMS, because the software itself had to be able to call up specific parts of the documentation. In a dynamic, responsive system such as the one envisioned by TypiComp's management, hypertext linking was a critical capability.

If TIMS contained 60,000 links, it would take 3,000 hours, or roughly a year and a half, to make the links — in a system based on content that was constantly changing!

The TIMS prototype team built these links by hand; they had to. There was nothing in the word processed source files that they could use to automate the task. This was fine for the prototype, but nobody did the math to see what that would mean for the production system. Links took an average of 3 minutes to construct. If TIMS ultimately contained 60,000 links, it would take 3,000 hours or roughly a year and a half of aggregated employee hours to make the links — a year and a half in a system based on content that was constantly changing to describe changes to the product!

Also, the TIMS team used the most recent set of documents that had been created in the technical documentation department — portions of the documentation for TypiComp's latest, and most impressive, system. But the department had used several different desktop publishing systems over the years, so they had some documents in the current product's format, and some in older formats. There were even some original — but still published — documents that existed only in print!

To make the TIMS team's life easier, Tom Spayling, the manager of technical documentation, had assigned a writer to "clean up" the sample documentation and put it all into the new format. So, unbeknownst to the TIMS prototypers, the sample document set they used was actually customized for their use. It did not reflect the real state of the documentation archives at TypiComp. Not even close.

Sixty thousand hypertext links, you're thinking? Messy, inconsistent word processing files? Not in *my* company. Well, if you think that, please go downstairs and take a look. I am *not* making this up.

Even with the cleansed source files, the TIMS team still spent an average of four hours per printed page reformatting the source for the online system. The software they were using required a different file format from the one the desktop publishing program used, and the content of the manual was going to be organized differently for TIMS. The technical documentation department estimated that there was approximately 4,000 printed pages of material that would eventually be included in TIMS. At four hours per, that was another 400 person/weeks worth of work.

But the team didn't really think about these issues. No one had asked them to do that. Their job was to build a prototype — to show TypiComp's management, board of directors, and customers what TIMS could be. And at that, they were a smashing success. Actually building the system was going to be somebody else's problem.

TIMS GETS REAL

Once management signed off on the prototype, the development of TIMS began in earnest. A development team was assembled to build the actual system.

After investigating the products available on the market, they selected a product called "FingerTip." FingerTip's marketing literature said it had everything they would need to create a fully interactive, state-of-the-art online information-delivery system. In particular, FingerTip offered filters that could "automatically convert documents from all the popular word processing programs" into online documents. There would be no hand building of links, no manual reformatting of pages. The team rejoiced; a computer would build TIMS from the already existing word processor files. The problem of all those hours spent creating links and reformatting pages would never become an issue.

Other users of FingerTip they contacted confirmed this — more or less. General consensus seemed to be that 70% to 80% of the conversion could be automated. The rest you did by hand. The development team figured they could live with this; FingerTip looked like the best option available.

GETTING TO THE SOURCE OF THE MATTER

The development team's first step was to assemble the files used to prepare TypiComp's printed manuals. So they went to the technical documentation department and requested them. Seemed like a simple request; they didn't expect this to be a problem.

To their surprise, Tom Spayling said that it would take several weeks to get "what we've got" together. "Everyone understands that TIMS is important," he said. "But we're already struggling to keep up with the work we have to do for the products that are under development. I don't have anybody that I can take off a project full time and devote to your work. There's no telling where all those files are right now. You are really going to need someone here to help you."

Development had not even started and they were already behind schedule.

As it turned out, having mixed file formats was only half the problem. Getting high-quality source files for TypiComp's printed documents turned out to be a real can of worms:

- TypiComp testbeds were usually refined right up to the day they shipped to the customer. In order to get as much information as possible into the printed manuals, final edits were often made directly to the copy of the document that was *at the print shop*. Although there was supposed to be a procedure for going back and making the same edits in the original word processor files, the reality was that, under the pressures of making the next deadline, the edits rarely got done. After all, how important was it that they be made? The right information was in the book and *that* was what mattered, wasn't it? So, the TIMS team learned right away that there were no guarantees that the content of the files exactly matched the content of the books, and there was no way to quickly track down what was different.

- There was no librarian in charge of maintaining the source files for TypiComp's manuals. While there was a published procedure for archiving the source files after a manual was finished, no one saw this as a crucial part of their job. The net result was that archiving was an ad hoc affair. Finding the source files that went with any given printed manual was hit-or-miss at best. The manager put out the word to the department that the

TIMS developers needed copies of the documentation files —
but there was no way to follow up, to make sure they delivered.
It was up to each writer to come through with his material.

■ TypiComp's older manuals — those that explained the basics of
using TypiComp systems — existed only on paper. They had
been produced many years back, when layout artists physically
pasted text and graphics onto boards. Those boards were in storage somewhere and there was *no* electronic source for the files.

The team was also surprised to discover how much of the information that had to be included in TIMS was written, produced, and
even distributed completely outside of the documentation department. Technical bulletins, release notes, and product descriptions were
written by engineers, product managers, and quality assurance testers,
and often these publications got out to customers through completely
different channels. *There was no one single place in the entire company
that acted as a central clearing house for the company's published information.* Just tracking down all these documents — important as they
were — was a job in itself, and, of course, they too turned out to exist
in a variety of different file formats.

Finally, the TIMS team discovered that, where the technical documentation gave information about subcomponent systems built by
outside suppliers, the information often reproduced the documents
supplied by the manufacturer. Again, electronic sources rarely existed,
and even when they did, the format and layout varied wildly from one
source to the next.

THE TROUBLE WITH TEXT

Finally, after a week of work, the team had assembled a critical mass
of information — not everything they would need to include in
TIMS, but enough to get started. Those manuals that existed only on

paper were out at a service bureau being rekeyed — an extra cost they had not budgeted for. Copies of the most recent files from customer service and quality assurance had been collected. All but the technical manuals currently being written were in hand. The team was ready to start work on the first iteration of TIMS.

Meanwhile, one of the team members had been playing around with FingerTip, the electronic publishing tool they had selected, learning its ins and outs. Turned out, there were a few to learn.

Those "automatic conversion filters" described in FingerTip's literature were not ready to run the minute you installed the product. Instead, they had to be "adjusted" — customized for each customer's file formats. And the "adjusting" required programming.

The reason customizing was needed was that no two organizations — or even writers, for that matter — use a word processor the same way. There are usually several different ways to get the same look on a piece of paper with any given word processing tool. So, although two printed pages may look the same, the underlying codes stored by the computer may be quite different. The conversion filters had to be modified to be able to recognize and correctly interpret the different variations in formatting that the writers produced.

This proved to be a much more involved process than the team had anticipated. The formatting from one manual to another turned out to be quite different. When they took this back to Tom Spayling, he acknowledged that "We have a style guide that's supposed to govern how writers format our books — but the writers don't always stick to it. Besides, am I going to fire a good writer just because he put something in italics instead of bold?"

There were problems even when the technical writer had followed the style guide to the letter. For example, one technical writer might indent paragraphs with the tab key, while another indented with spaces. One writer might use the product's table function to create tables, while another spaced the columns out by hand.

This was an especially big headache when it came to the cross references, those "For more information . . . " type phrases that were supposed to be turned into hypertext links automatically. The writers could express a cross reference in an astonishingly large number of ways: "For more information, see page . . ." and "See section . . . for more information" and "This is further described in section . . ." and, everyone's favorite ". . . as described above." Some of the writers had pointed their readers to specific pages, some to the subsection, and some just to the chapter. And, as in the "described above" case, it was not always clear what the writer was pointing to, unless the reader was consuming the book from cover to cover. Tweaking the automatic conversion filters to handle all these variations turned out to be one of the major efforts of the project. The team member responsible for programming the FingerTip filter likened it to "building an artificial intelligence program *and* a grammar checker from scratch!"

These problems were only compounded for the other publications, such as technical bulletins, where almost every document was different.

THE 101ST-PAGE PARADOX

After working on a subset of 100 pages, the team felt that they had accounted for enough of the vagaries of formatting and phrasing to enable them to do a test run on one of the manuals. They pulled all the components of the first 500-page document together, fed them to FingerTip and sat back.

On page 101, the program crashed.

It turned out that the conversion filter ran into a bulleted list. Normally, that would not have been a problem, but this one happened to be inside a numbered list that was inside a table. No one had anticipated finding anything that complex inside the document.

The team now revised its game plan. They sat down with this 500-page book and they pored over it, looking at how each different component was formatted. They found that bulleted lists had been done 16 different ways. They found tables done 9 different ways, including one chapter that was a gigantic table from start to finish! They found equations done using the word processor's equation-writing tool and equations done as little pictures. They found constructions in different parts of the book that were clearly procedures but that were formatted very differently. Clearly, using formatting tools to create documents was resulting in files that caused major problems for the TIMS team.

After some experimentation and development, they came up with a workable solution. They developed FingerTip conversion filters that included flags to mark the places where the conversion filter could not recognize the input. If the conversion filter ran into formatting that it could not recognize, it treated it as a hypertext link to the error index. This was actually pretty clever. The conversion process almost never crashed, and, after running a document through the filter, the developer ended up with an electronic book that included a list of 'I-don't-knows' at the end. The developer could go down that list, jump back to the source of the problem, figure out what was wrong, and fix it in the source file. The second time through, the book would usually be completely clean.

And they found that, yes, just as other customers had told them, 70% to 80% of the process was automated, leaving 20% to 30% that had to be done by hand. Unfortunately, they now understood that this meant that 20% to 30% was going to have to be done *every time* they added new or revised documents to TIMS. Developing TIMS systems to go on each testbed TypiComp produced was never going to be a push-button operation. There would always be some amount of manual labor, delay, and extra expense involved.

In the end, they fielded a TIMS system. It was six months later than promised, did not have as much content as they had originally intended to put in, and was not quite as visionary a product as they had envisioned. For example, they never did get it integrated into an automated diagnostic system. Although they were able to prototype a sample diagnostic system, it required so much custom work to build that they didn't think they could ever field a commercially viable version.

But even in its limited form, TIMS was well received by staff and customers. In truth, it represented a quality-of-life improvement for everyone who used TypiComp's documentation. And everyone was satisfied with the result, until the day just recently when Sam walked into Margaret's office and asked her what it would take to make TIMS available over the World Wide Web.

But *that's* a story for another time.

If TypiComp had looked into SGML, they would have discovered a technique for storing information that would have let them build TIMS so that it was all that they had imagined.

WHAT WENT WRONG?

If we accept for the moment that TypiComp's vision of TIMS was not idealistic, naive, or blue sky — and trust me on this, it wasn't — then why did they have so much trouble building the system they wanted? It wasn't because the company wasn't willing to spend money on a worthwhile project. And it wasn't because they shortchanged the project on intellectual capital.

No, TIMS was really hobbled by two fundamental misunderstandings:

1. No one realized how useless the formatting commands inside their word processing files would be for computerized processing beyond getting a sheet of paper out of a printer.

2. No one realized how many different groups at TypiComp were creating and distributing vital documents following their own ad hoc procedures — often without even knowing of one another's existence.

In order to build a system like TIMS, you have to be able to let the computer do the work. Those cross-reference links, for example, that would take human operators 3,000 hours to build by hand (and just as many hours to change if you decided to reorganize the system) can take today's average laptop just a few minutes to create — *if* the computer can tell which text is a link and what it has to link to.

And those automatic hooks between diagnostic systems running on the testbed and the relevant repair procedures in the manuals can be built automatically, *if* the computer can tell repair procedures from other numbered lists that are formatted the same way — say, parts lists or the questions on the customer-satisfaction survey.

But what's stored inside the typical WYSIWYG word processor file tells the computer nothing about what the text is or what could be done with it. What's stored are commands that tell the computer how to make the words print out on paper — and nothing else! A repair procedure, for example, will have formatting commands that determine the typeface, and then a number, followed by some indented text. Same as the parts list. Same as the questionnaire. Same as every other numbered list that is included in the document.

TypiComp found out, just as other companies find out every day, that appearances can be deceiving. TypiComp's managers and engineers made the understandable mistake of assuming that, because they could see a representation of a printed page on their computer screens, they therefore had some sort of data in the computer that the computer could manipulate for other purposes.

This is where SGML comes in. If TypiComp had looked into SGML, they would have discovered a technique for defining and storing information about the identity and meaning of the document's contents instead of its appearance. They would have found an approach to documents that is designed to support both human and computer processing of documents. They would have found the tool that would have let them build TIMS so that it could be all that they had imagined.

TypiComp and the TIMS team learned this truth the hard way. Most companies do. We are all still early in the learning curve, changing from the world where we moved paper to a world where we move information. Fortunately for us all, some organizations have taken the first steps already. In the remaining chapters of this book, you're going to hear *their* stories. These stories have very different outcomes from TypiComp's.

CHAPTER 3

Grolier, Incorporated

*The data in an encyclopedia is very long lived, but
over the years visual taste changes dramatically. You must
build systems that support the data, not today's fashions.*

— Larry Lorimer, Vice President & Editor-In-Chief,
Editorial Reference Division

EXECUTIVE SUMMARY

THE GROUP

Editorial Reference Division.

THEIR MISSION

To create and maintain the content for major reference works including the *Encyclopedia Americana*, the *Academic American Encyclopedia*, and the *New Book of Knowledge*.

TYPE OF APPLICATION

Information database.

SUMMARY

Many companies have collected large reservoirs of valuable knowledge in documents. What distinguishes a company like Grolier is that the reservoir is also their product. For example, their three main encyclopedias have over 50,000 printed pages and over 90,000 articles covering every aspect of human knowledge. This is highly interconnected information — the the *Encyclopedia Americana* alone has over 100,000 direct cross references between articles.

In 1985, Grolier published the the *Grolier Electronic Encyclopedia*, the first general reference publication made available on CD-ROM. Since then, Grolier has continued to find innovative ways to republish their content for new distribution channels. But Grolier's manual editorial systems, which were adequate when new editions of the encyclopedia were published once a year, could not keep pace with the demands of a publishing environment that needed to have all its information accurate and up to date at all times. In 1990, Grolier set out to build a system that would let the editorial staff support the demands of real-time publishing.

Today, Grolier maintains the source data for their print, CD-ROM, and online products in SGML. Many of the manual tasks that had been productivity killers have been automated; editors can now keep articles up to date all the time.

Grolier has realized benefits above and beyond those that they deliberately set out to achieve. Editors can now quickly locate other articles that may be affected by a change to the current article, and they can see the impact that a change will have on the print or electronic version, two things that were previously impossible. And they have found that their content has a depth it never had before. By defining information elements explicitly in the SGML files, Grolier can develop new products and enhance existing ones far faster than they could if their data was in a page-oriented database.

THE ORIGINAL DATABASE: GROLIER, INCORPORATED

Picture this: It is 7:00 p.m. on a winter's evening in November, 1989. You are the editor-in-chief for an encyclopedia publishing company and your staff is hard at work on the next edition of your encyclopedia. You have a master revision plan that details all the changes to be made for the next edition and a production schedule that you've kept to so far. Everyone on your staff knows what they have to do. Now, after a long day at the office, you are home watching the evening news and you are seeing thousands of people tear down the Berlin Wall with their hands.

As a citizen of the world, you are happy for this dramatic turn of events. But as the leader of a group responsible for keeping 27,000 pages of knowledge up to date, you are steeling yourself for weeks of grueling work. Because the world has just thrown your plan, your schedule, and your vacation right out the window.

You consider the encyclopedia on which you work. Its 27,000 pages contain more than 45,000 articles. In those articles are some 100,000 cross references to other articles, 12,000 photos, maps, and charts, 700 statistical "fact boxes," and 6,000 bibliographies. You have no automated system that can tell you how many of these have just been rendered out of date.

Obviously, articles on Germany and Berlin will have to be edited. Articles on the United States and the USSR may need changes, too. But what else has been affected? The article on communism? The article on the cold war? How many biographies have to change? How many of those maps, photos, fact boxes, or bibliographies are now obsolete? There is no way to know for sure unless you and your staff inspect all 27,000 pages.

It begins to look like you could stop work on everything else and spend the rest of your schedule just trying to incorporate this political change into the encyclopedia. That, or resign yourself to fixing only the most obvious errors and publishing the encyclopedia with an unknown number of inaccuracies — inaccuracies that will persist for years to come.

The scenario may sound discouraging, but it illustrates the problems encyclopedia publishers have faced for centuries. Even the advent of the computer did little to change the industry's operating procedures. Then, in 1990, Grolier, Incorporated decided that it was time to look for a better way.

THE BUSINESS CHALLENGE

The variety of distribution channels give Grolier a significant presence in the marketplace. It also puts significant pressure on the editorial staff to keep the vast store of content current.

Grolier publishes encyclopedias, children's books, and other educational materials, both on paper and electronically. Founded at the turn of the century, today Grolier is part of the Lagardère Groupe, an international technology, manufacturing, and media company based in France.

Grolier's premier products are its three encyclopedias: the in-depth *Encyclopedia Americana*; the *Academic American Encyclopedia*, a short-entry encyclopedia oriented toward middle and high school students, and *The New Book of Knowledge*, aimed at children. Grolier was the first reference publisher to sell its information electronically, beginning in the 1980s with the first online services. In 1985, Grolier released *The Grolier Multimedia Encyclopedia*, the first encyclopedia to be published on CD-ROM.

Grolier continues to find innovative ways to capitalize on its copyrighted content. Today, Grolier offers the *Encyclopedia Americana* as well as the *The Grolier Multimedia Encyclopedia* on CD-ROM. It also publishes other reference and edutainment titles including *Prehistoria*, *The Guinness Multimedia Disc of Records*, and *The Encyclopedia of Science Fiction*.

The *Academic American Encyclopedia* is also available on CompuServe and America Online, the international online services. With the 1996 edition of *The Grolier Multimedia Encyclopedia*, readers with

CompuServe accounts can automatically link from an article stored on the CD to CompuServe for updated articles and related information.

This variety of distribution channels and access methods gives Grolier a significant presence and competitive advantage in the marketplace for reference products. It also puts significant pressure on the editorial staff to keep the vast store of content current

Figure 3–1. Grolier's product line includes CD-ROM editions of their flagship "Encyclopedia Americana." *Courtesy of Grolier, Inc.*

and accurate. Publishing out-of-date information is not an option when the very sort of event that makes the most work for the editors — the collapse of the Soviet Union or the discovery of buckyballs — is the same sort of event that brings readers flocking to your door.

PUBLISHING THE "ORIGINAL DATABASE"

The problem is common to every business: constrained resources. The real challenge was to build a system that would help them accomplish more within the limits of these constraints.

If you want to be this innovative with your data, you can't afford a system that holds your people back. As early as 1989, everyone from the president on down could see that the systems for managing Grolier's huge store of information would have to change. They were too slow and cumbersome to meet the demands of the times.

In 1990, Grolier's senior management made a strategic decision to develop computer-based systems to support publishing. The decision was a logical next step in keeping with Grolier's corporate commitment of providing a more diverse and targeted set of products to their primary market. Grolier management established the *Computerization Task Force*, a group that included the president, the vice presidents of publishing, information services, and manufacturing, the CFO, and Larry Lorimer, the new vice president and editor-in-chief of the Editorial Reference Division. It was Larry's job to figure out what this new system would be.

At first, Larry Lorimer doesn't strike you as the sort of fellow who would be sitting on the cutting edge of a technology revolution. He speaks in quiet, measured tones (which belie his obvious enthusiasm), not about PCs or CD-ROM drives or surfing the Internet, but rather about the unique nature of the problems that anyone who wants to improve encyclopedia publishing must solve.

"Encyclopedias are interesting animals," he says. "When you think about it, the encyclopedia was really the first database. People here were already very data sensitive without being at all technological."

Being anything but transfixed by machines and flashy software, Larry
and his staff instead could focus their attention on the real nature of
the problem.

Larry knew that any computer system that was going to help the
editors publish both print *and* electronic reference books was going to
have to be able to handle the rather unique problems of encyclopedia
publishing.

"An encyclopedia is a container of fixed size; its page count can't
expand to accommodate new information," Larry says. If that strikes
you as odd, consider how much it would cost to completely replace
the plates used to print a 27,000-page encyclopedia. The words "pro-
hibitively expensive" immediately come to mind. Instead, each year,
the publisher sets a budget for the number of pages that can be
changed for that edition. The rest are reprinted from the existing
plates. Larry smiles as he sets up the problem this creates.

"Now Bill Clinton is elected President. And there is only one place
in the encyclopedia where 'Clinton, William' can go. So editors have
to start asking themselves questions. How much information about
Bill Clinton are they going to put in? What information are they
going to cut around it to make it fit? What else will they have to
change? The articles on Arkansas or the Democratic Party? And what
will they cut around those articles?" (See Figure 3–2).

But what about the electronic editions? That makes the challenge
"somewhat more complicated," Larry says. "The group that publishes
the electronic versions of the encyclopedia does not have these space
limitations. They want to include all the information they can get. So
we have to be able to distinguish edits made for copyfitting from edits
made to correct or update information." In other words, the cuts an
editor makes to fit copy in the printed version shouldn't really be *cut*
at all; they must be kept in the publishing database but somehow
marked so that they are not used in the paper version.

As if that weren't enough to keep everyone busy, consider this: you
are also working with information that has an enormous number of

Figure 3–2. Grolier editors must fit new articles into the encyclopedia with minimum impact on surrounding pages.

interdependencies and cross connections. The fall of the Berlin Wall and the collapse of the Soviet Union are just extreme examples of what happens to editors every day.

The direct connections between articles are staggering enough; the *Academic American Encyclopedia* has more than 67,000 cross references, the *Encyclopedia Americana* over 100,000. If you decide to delete an article, how can you know whether or not it is referenced from other articles in the encyclopedia?

The indirect interdependencies are even worse. Facts, statistics, and common wisdom do not occur just once in the encyclopedia; they can be repeated over and over in a number of articles, each with its own different slant. The number of distinct bird species in North America may be mentioned in the article about birds, in articles on individual species of birds, in the article about North America, and the article about the environmental movement. Under the paper-based systems, there was no reliable way to track all these references down. Larry remembers that "I'd ask the editors-in-chief how many articles they had on birds and they'd answer, 'Oh, quite a few.' I'd ask them how many *pages* they had on birds and they had even less of an idea."

The problem is common to every business in the world: constrained resources. Encyclopedia editors are paid to make value judgments about what facts or subjects get more attention or less and to keep their subject matter current. But they have to base their decisions not only on editorial values and philosophy but also on the physical restrictions of the page count and available time. Larry knew that the real challenge to automating the process was to build these people a system that would help them accomplish more within the limits of these constraints.

MORE THAN A HARDWARE PROBLEM

As a first step toward automation, Grolier put a PC on every editor's desk. This was useful to the extent that editors started getting some experience with desktop computing. Larry gave Cyndie Cooper, his newly hired director of editorial electronics, the job of figuring out what else was needed.

Cyndie looked around the editorial department and what did she see? Fifty-plus smart, capable people using high-powered personal computers as fast typewriters. "The editors were using their PCs to write new articles, but everything else was still being done the old way."

And the old way was pretty labor intensive. Tearsheets — pages taken from the last published version of the encyclopedia — were pasted onto large sheets of paper and given to the editors. They wrote minor edits into the blank area to the right of the page. Major revisions were sent out to be typeset. Since it was critically important to control the number of lines, artists in the department would make mockups of the revised page to show the editors how their changes would fit.

These mockups were no guarantee, however, that the page that eventually came back from the typesetter would turn out as the editor expected. Fitting printed copy into a space is not as simple as counting letters or words. Believe it or not, words and the space around them can be of different sizes on a printed page, depending on how many other words are on the line with them. This is part of the art of typesetting. The only way to know for certain how the final printed page will look is to make it and see. So some articles went from a Grolier editor to the typesetter several times just to get the fit right. "We were bound up by the print constraints. There were six weeks minimum being lost in the outside production loop. Content had to go out to be typeset before editors could know for certain that the line or two they had cut would paginate properly," Cyndie explains.

And meanwhile, the electronic publishing team was using those marked-up tearsheets *to type the copyfitting edits back in again!* Grolier was taking a double productivity hit!

It was obvious that simply putting machines on everyone's desk didn't make anything happen faster. There was a complex manufacturing process at work here, and any system that was going to automate it would have to reflect what that process really was.

UNDERSTANDING THE PROCESS

"We inherited an extraordinarily *methodical* engine for producing encyclopedias," Larry explains. "It was well oiled, smoothly running — if anything, it was too organized." The checks and balances were intricate and tightly woven, which only made the process of introducing supporting technology all the more exacting.

Cyndie explains, "I realized that before I could design anything, I needed to understand reference information and reference publishing. What are the dependencies? How does this environment work?" To do that, and to get the staff involved in the development of the new system, Cyndie gathered together a study group. The group had 15 people, including representatives from every area that would be touched by the new system, both inside the division and out. Cyndie and Larry both felt strongly that "If we didn't have a user base committed to this system, we'd be lost."

They had good reason to be concerned. Vane Lashua, the current director of editorial electronics, recalls, "The introduction of the PC into the publishing industry had not been a friendly transition. Too many publishing houses tried to use it as a way to cut staff, and the PC got a bad reputation with publishing professionals." But that was not the goal at Grolier, and it was important that everyone knew it. "We were already short staffed," Cyndie says. "The reason for bringing in a new system was to help people be more productive and to be able to produce new products more cost effectively. So it was important to us to let everybody know that the *way* they did their jobs was going to change but we weren't looking to downsize."

Larry emphasizes this point: "We stayed very conscious that this system we were trying to build had to be an *environment* that our people could work in without feeling that they'd been made into automated technicians." Not a computer system, but rather an environment that supports the job, the process. That's worth remembering.

With her study group in place, Cyndie took rolls of brown wrapping paper and hung them up all around the walls of her office. "And then we started to chart the process." Members of the team would come into Cyndie's office and talk through the part of the process that they were scrutinizing. They would ask each other questions like: "What do you do with this piece of information? Where does it go after it leaves your hands?" And the especially important question "*Why* do you do what you do with it?" (See Figure 3–3).

"We stayed very conscious that this system had to be an environment that our people could work in without feeling that they'd been made into automated technicians."

—Larry Lorimer

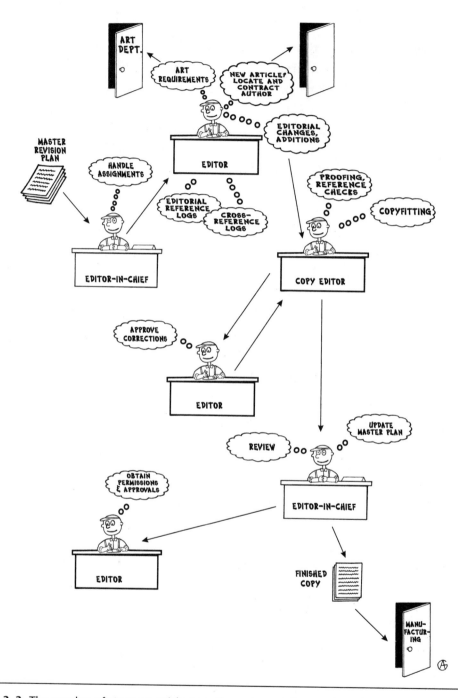

Figure 3–3. The number of steps an article goes through, and the number of people who work on it, can be substantial.

The payoff began right off the bat. Members of the study group began to discover procedures and processes that had been in place for so long that everyone had forgotten why they were doing things that way. In one situation, the production editor was making five different copies of a page and sending them to five different people. When asked what those people did with their copies, no one knew. They pulled in those five people one by one and learned that they no longer did anything with the copies. They were either filing them or throwing them away. So this whole step was eliminated.

AND DEFINING THE OBJECTIVES

Once the different groups were familiar with each other's problems and issues and began to appreciate the overall process, they began to construct a conceptual plan. Cyndie: "We could finally say what it was we wanted."

Cyndie asked everyone on the study team to think, not just about their present problems, but also about the future. She asked them to think about what they wanted the new system to do. She asked them to think about what new business problems the solution would produce. She asked them to think about the new business model the system would create. For example, they were working at that time on a yearly update cycle; the editors changed content only when they were preparing the next edition of an encyclopedia. The new system would allow them to update the information in the articles constantly. How would that affect the process and the organization? What could they do now that they hadn't been able to do before? What would they have to do differently?

From the original study team, Cyndie chose a group to write the conclusions and recommendations into a formal Request For Proposal that they could take to the vendors. In writing the RFP, they decided to focus on the functions and capabilities they needed — what they called 'strategic goals' — and not specify technology. They doubted any one vendor would have the perfect system, so they wanted to enable the developers to be creative in their proposals. The one technology requirement explicitly stated was that the system support SGML.

WHY SGML?

In the early '90s, not a lot of people were using SGML. Cyndie recalls that making the decision to go with SGML was a bit scary. "We believed that SGML as a solution was the right choice. But as a practical technology, there were not many products on the market, and most were sold by small, relatively new companies that might not survive." So why base the new system on an open standard like SGML? Weren't there proprietary systems that could solve their problems?

There may have been. But Cyndie's experiences with proprietary publishing systems had left a lasting impression. "I had worked for the technical publications department at a major telecommunications equipment manufacturing company that was determined to stay on the cutting edge of the technology. We were always buying new products and getting involved in major file conversions, even while we were in the middle of active projects. It was a nightmare."

A word of explanation: Converting from one word processing or composition program's format to another is never a 100% automatic process. Different products always have different capabilities. One may be able to print text on an angle, the other may not. One may be able to wrap text around pictures, the other may not. Also, the more powerful the program, the more ways it gives users to create these effects. The automatic conversion program has yet to be written that knows all the nuances of all the formatting capabilities of all the possible combinations of programs out there, or that knows what to do with that sideways or wrap-around text when the product it is trying to convert to doesn't support it.

The problem is even worse than that. There is not even an automatic way to find all the trouble spots and flag them for human review. The only reliable way to do that is for someone to look at every page — a real productivity killer! Cyndie had lived through it all, and she promised herself that "if there was any way to avoid those kinds of data conversions here at Grolier, I'd do it."

Proprietary solutions have another drawback as well. The problem that today's program solves for you is not the problem that you have to solve tomorrow. Today, your problem may be automating the publication of your 27,000 pieces of paper, and this program may be great for that. But tomorrow, your problem may be identifying and extracting all the science-related articles for a new specialty product. Or it may be publishing your encyclopedia on the World Wide Web. And suddenly you are faced with one of those ugly conversions described above, because your proprietary system doesn't do that. So you have to redo all the content in a system that does.

One of the key objectives for Grolier's new system, as stated in the RFP, was to "provide the resources for development of new print and electronic products through reuse of existing materials and efficient preparation of new elements." Larry, Cyndie, and the reference staff were not about to settle on a solution that potentially limited their future options. They had already decided that, as Cyndie put it, "It's better to look a little bit further into the future, than to just try and solve today's business problem."

Larry and Cyndie knew that SGML, because it stores information about a document's structure instead of its appearance, would avoid the problems inherent in proprietary systems. Processing SGML documents into different formats can be automated, because it is largely a process of mapping the known structure of the SGML data to the format codes used by the publishing program, be it for paper or electronic output. Flagging problems for human review can be automated, because the SGML itself is predictable. If required data is missing or if it occurs in the wrong place in the data stream, it can be flagged for review.

SGML also solved the problem of being prepared for tomorrow's challenges. Computer programs could be written that would process the SGML markup into the form needed for whatever form of reuse they would want in the future. SGML offered them a process-neutral way to develop new products and outputs quickly. For all these reasons, SGML was the right solution.

Now the only question was whether or not a vendor could deliver a system based on it.

TAKING THE OBJECTIVES TO THE MANUFACTURERS

In March of 1991, Grolier sent out the Request For Proposal for vendor review. They held a vendor conference in May. At that meeting, they reviewed the RFP with the assembled vendors and fielded questions.

To their surprise, the vendors didn't ask many. Most of them seemed to have attended in order to see who else was there. Members of the study groups and other Grolier people had been sprinkled throughout the audience, mostly to be able to answer questions and help out with the presentation. But they overheard plenty of comments, most falling into the general category of "These people must be nuts!" As the vendors left, Larry and Cyndie pondered how many of them were likely to return.

In the end, they got what they considered five serious bids. After benchmarking trials and system architecture reviews, it was clear that they had been right. No company had a complete solution. Larry and Cyndie choose to go with the company that seemed to understand their problems best and that was closest to having a solution that fit. The company brought in other vendors to handle the components that they themselves did not produce. "That's another advantage of an open architecture." Cyndie says. "You can pick the vendors with the best product for each part of the puzzle."

Then everybody got to work.

CONVERTING 27,000 PAGES TO SGML

For an SGML project, converting libraries of existing documents — called "legacy data" in the trade — into SGML can be one of the biggest parts of the entire undertaking. Grolier was no exception.

Larry recalls that "When we first decided that we were going to move to some sort of electronic system based on SGML, we started getting the data into an electronic format. And of course, we chose the *mother* of all encyclopedias, the *Encyclopedia Americana*, to start with." One reason they picked it was that, on first inspection, it appeared to be page after page of text following a simple design, unlike the more graphically rich pages of the *Academic American Encyclopedia* or the *New Book of Knowledge*. In other words, it looked like it would be easy. "It was only when we got into it that we realized how painfully structurally deep the information was."

Consider, for example, a name. On the page, the name of the person — say, for example "Andrew Jackson, 7th President of the United States" — may be printed in bold. Certainly, SGML would allow you to mark it as bold text. But that would be repeating the mistake made by proprietary programs. There are advantages to having the text stored in the underlying data structure not as bold text, but as a name.

Once a name is identified as a name, you can write computer programs to do useful things with it (see Figure 3–4). For example, you can write a program that automatically builds family genealogies and refers the reader to biographies, where they exist. You can write a program that links references to the person in other parts of the encyclopedia to his biography, even though in one article the person is referred to as "Andrew Jackson," in another as "President Jackson," and in yet a third as "Old Hickory." (You could do this by hand, too. It would just take longer. Much, much longer.)

It was analyses like these, made as they developed the SGML structure, that made the superficially simple *Encyclopedia Americana* become more and more complicated as they went forward. Or, should I say, more and more rich. Grolier developed their DTD[1] with the help of an outside consultant, in the process identifying useful element types such as *name, location, pronunciation, author affiliation, fact box,* and *map* as important components of the encyclopedia that would be useful for subsequent processing of the information.

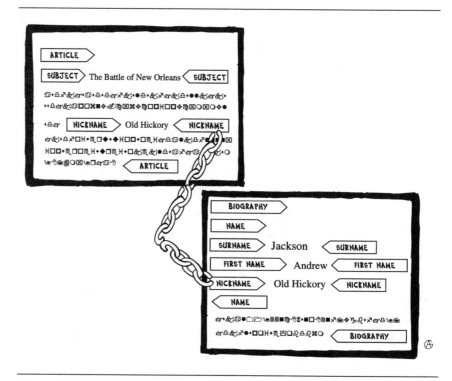

Figure 3–4. When the elements of a name are identified in the data, linking occurrences in different locations can be done automatically.

They had the encyclopedia's contents retyped overseas using a simple DTD created expressly for this task with the expectation that they would enhance the information content later. They debated

---

1 Document type definition, or DTD, is described in Chapter 1.

whether to add additional SGML "smarts" to the information immediately or do it gradually, as articles came up for revision in the paper
publishing cycle. Larry recalls that "For some business reason, long
since lost to memory, we thought that we were going to have to use
the data quickly to put out a new product." So they decided to deal
with the content all at once. "As it turned out, we didn't do the new
product, but the pressure was a fortunate thing for us. If we had not
done the entire *Americana* at once, we would still be migrating to
SGML today."

Of course, the benefit of an SGML conversion is that you incur
this conversion cost one time and then automate your conversions for
future outputs. A conversion from a formatting program to SGML
may be as difficult as a conversion to another formatting program —
one of those ugly conversions described earlier. But the benefit is that
you won't have to go through the experience again when the next
product comes along.

IMPLEMENTING THE SYSTEM

Once the vendor was chosen, the system came together quickly.
The network was installed in January of 1992. Testing and training
for the new editorial system began in May. The first page composed
for the *Encyclopedia Americana* rolled off the system in July. They
had been working under the burden of a paper-centric system for a
long time and they wanted to see the promise of the new system put
into practice.

Grolier handled training internally. They held a two-day class to
introduce the staff to SGML concepts. They followed up with three
days of training on the editorial system, using Grolier data as samples.
Two technical-support people were dedicated to help the editorial staff
for the first two weeks. After that, the editorial staff took it largely on
their own.

Cyndie recalls that introducing SGML to the staff was an interesting experience. At first, it was frustrating. "The editors came from a background that was print and format oriented. They would ask, 'Why are you making us do all this extra work? Why do we have to mark up a family name, a given name, a nickname, when we just want them to be bold or italic?'"[2]

Cyndie felt like she'd been over it all one hundred times: how Grolier would be able to spin off new products, build richer, more interactive CD-ROMs, change the look and feel of the material quickly, and so on. It wasn't until the editors got the "article preview" function that she could see the 'aha' light go on in their heads.

"We had built an 'article preview' function," Cyndie says "and we had made it a menu option on the editing system." The article preview sent the article that the editor was working on to the automated composition system. It returned a preview of how the article would look once it was in the encyclopedia. Unlike the old page mockup process, this utility showed exactly how lines of text in the final article would break, so the editors could instantly tell how edits to an article would affect the articles and pages around it. Also unlike the old process, this took moments instead of days. Cyndie says "They went gaga over it. We would be in these meetings where the staff were all saying 'This is terrific!' and we would just sit there like the cat that ate the canary."

THE PAYOFF

Larry, Cyndie, and the Grolier staff built the SGML foundation they envisioned. They automated many of the old productivity killers — laborious production chores that stole time from value-adding creative

---

2 *README.1ST: SGML for Writers and Editors* answers precisely these questions for precisely this audience. Unfortunately, it wasn't available in 1992.

work. And they added a new dimension of "intellectual rigor and discipline." "Today we add intelligent structure to the encyclopedia," Larry says, "instead of just changing the look of the page."

Grolier has realized significant benefits from adopting SGML:

■ **One group of editors — and one document database — support a stream of paper and electronic products without the constant retyping, reformatting, rewriting, and reorganizing that other formats would require.**

"We didn't justify the system by saying "Someday we'll be able to do an electronic encyclopedia," Larry says. "We were already doing that. Now we have our data in a form that lets us do new products quickly and efficiently. Other companies have to start from zero.""

Since Grolier's adoption of SGML, the *Encyclopedia Americana* has joined the *Grolier Multimedia Encyclopedia* as a CD-ROM product. The developer reports that because the content was represented in SGML, Grolier saved over $100,000 in development costs and dramatically shortened the time to market.

Grolier saved over $100,000 in development costs and dramatically shortened the time to market.

The editors can also keep customizations and tweaks to the content of any one product in the same source document. Articles that exist only in the electronic editions of the encyclopedias — either because they were cut for copyfitting purposes or because the editors thought readers of the electronic product would be interested in them — remain part of the overall document database. The same is true for variations between the article in print and the article online. "The text of the print and electronic encyclopedias started to diverge almost immediately," Larry remembers. "Rather than trying to prevent that from happening, we built the system to support it."

■ **The editors can finally keep *all* the information in the encyclopedia current and up to date.**

Yesterday, they had to rely on a time-consuming, labor-intensive, and less-than-100%-reliable catalog of index cards to keep track of cross references and correlation between articles. If someone, under the pressure of an impending deadline, didn't record a change on the cards, the integrity of the catalog was compromised. And since those sorts of human errors were inevitable, everyone was resigned to the fact that the encyclopedia would have a certain number of references in it that were broken.

Today, an editor can get a report that shows all the references to an article throughout the encyclopedia. The task of locating cross references has become an automated task handled by the computer.

Interdependencies among diverse articles can be managed as well. When editors change content, they can search the structure of the encyclopedia to find related articles that must also change. Cyndie recalls that "When the Soviet Union disintegrated, there would have been no way the editors could have found all the thousands and thousands of references to the USSR scattered all over the encyclopedia." Larry adds, "We would still be finding errors and fixing them."

- **They have been able to use SGML and the technology of the World Wide Web to streamline a number of internal business processes.**

World Wide Web documents are coded in a format called HyperText Markup Language, or HTML. Normally, an organization that wants to make information available over the Web must create or convert documents to HTML and store them separately from the original documents. However, HTML is simply another application of SGML. Grolier has discovered that they can transform many of their information resources into HTML automatically and use Web browsers as a universal business tool.

For example, they now use Web browsers as the tool for tracking graphics. Many of the articles in the encyclopedias have graphics — photographs, illustrations, maps, and so on. Each graphic has to be assigned a unique tracking number so that it can be managed throughout the production process. In the past, they had to record these numbers in paper log books, and, because of the high volume of graphics that Grolier's editorial staff works with, the books were hard to keep up to date.

Because the illustrations are all unambiguously identified as SGML elements, Vane Lashua's staff wrote a program that extracted all existing graphics and their tracking numbers into a database. All the editors can access the database using a Web browser right from their desktop. Now, instead of having to stop what they are doing and leave their desk in order to submit an illustration request form and register a number, they can handle the whole process on the spot. "The paper log book was always out of date," Vane says. "The online log is always up to date."

Grolier has also used Web technology to put the current contents of the encyclopedias at the editors' fingertips. "We wrote a program that converts our SGML into HTML on the fly," Vane explains. "Whenever an editor wants to check on the current content of an article, he simply runs the Web browser on his PC and calls up the article. The program creates the HTML as it sends the article to him." The editors always have immediate access to the current version of any article, yet Grolier does not have tie up resources keeping a duplicate copy of the article on their system. "This simply wouldn't be feasible if we had to keep storing copies of articles in HTML every time we changed them," Vane explains.

The technologies used by the Internet and the World Wide Web are terrific tools for internal business communications. But many companies have to factor the cost of data conversion into their decisionmaking when considering the possibilities. Grolier's

The World Wide Web is terrific for internal business communications. But many companies have to factor the cost of data conversion into their decision-making. Grolier's SGML is tailor-made for this environment.

SGML data is tailor-made for this environment, and they continue to find ways to take advantage of it. "We are getting better and better at thinking of ways to make things simpler," Vane concludes.

- **Grolier has dramatically cut its prepress costs.**

It wasn't that they wanted to take on page layout; they had to. The editors were losing roughly six weeks of their production time to outside composition loops. Now the editors can select a menu option and immediately see the impact of edits on the composed page. Instead of rekeying and typesetting printed pages, the printers work with electronic copies of pages produced at Grolier. They create the plates for the printing presses directly from those files.

This has had a subtle impact on the editors' productivity as well. They no longer have to put an article on hold for weeks while they wait for the composed page to come back. Before, if the page wasn't right, they would have to get reoriented to what they had been doing and thinking when they made the edit the first time. Now, they can wrap up the edits to an article on the spot.

- **They have streamlined the editorial operation and improved their ability to measure its outputs.**

Earlier in this story, we saw how the simple act of charting all the steps involved in the editorial process on Cyndie's brown-paper-covered walls revealed procedures that could change and steps that could be eliminated. It revealed something else as well.

"We realized early on that we faced a major obstacle — the department had no statistics," Cyndie recalls. Because all their information was imprisoned on paper — paper that busy people had to spend time moving from place to place — there was no way the system could capture the kinds of performance-measuring information you would want to have. No way to tell how long it took to process a photo request. No way to tell how long it took to finish revisions to an article. No way even to know for sure how many articles the encyclopedia contained!

Because the data now resides in an SGML structure that identifies things like articles, and subject classifications, Grolier editors can measure the output of their work far more precisely. The system can count the number of articles, tables, bibliographies, and so on contained in an edition of the encyclopedia. Not only do they have better, more accurate statistical information than they had before, they also have a solid foundation for building project-management systems that rely on the computer — instead of people — to control the workload and schedules in the department.

■ **They have better control over the individual data types that go into the encyclopedia than ever before.**

This is no small point. There is a lot of stuff that goes into an encyclopedia besides the body of the articles: maps, photos, chronologies, graphics of flags and seals — the list goes on and on. The *New Book of Knowledge,* Grolier's children's encyclopedia, looks downright magazine-ish at some points. Making sure that all the pieces ended up where they belonged used to burn up a lot of editorial hours. Today it is a nonissue.

Characters and symbols posed a similar problem when Grolier first began publishing electronically. There are over 200 separate characters in the encyclopedia. The English alphabet, the digits 0 through 9, and standard punctuation account for 64 of them. What are the other 136? Foreign-language characters, special punctuation characters, and a host of exotic mathematical symbols and other types of glyphs.

And every computer system stores them differently. Because they are rarely used, the only way to be certain that these types of characters were being printed or displayed properly was to proofread the finished product. Now, however, the characters are stored in a generic form specified by SGML. The generic form can be mapped to the specific format required for each system when the data is processed, and the editorial group can be assured that those special characters will be reproduced as reliably as the English alphabet.

- **SGML has given a depth to their data far beyond what they originally expected.**

As they analyzed the content of the encyclopedia, they realized that there was a lot of metadata — information *about* the articles — that they wanted to keep and use: the article's primary subject discipline and subdiscipline categories, the date the article was last reviewed or updated, the reason a change was made and the source of the information used to change it, and so on. Consider, as an example, an editor making a change to the article on Brazil, based on information from *The CIA Worldbook*. If someone later challenges the accuracy of that change, it is very valuable to be able to point back to the original source as justification.

Keeping this kind of information associated with the article would have been difficult to do with most proprietary systems. With SGML, the Grolier staff was able to define its own metadata types and store that information directly with the article. They originally identified a list of 28 key metadata elements that they wanted to store with the article, but the list grew as they continued to define their requirements and gain more experience with using the system. A key advantage of SGML has been the ability to continue to enhance the content of the data over time — something that would be almost impossible to do without SGML.

Is there more to do? Of course. A system of this magnitude is a living thing; it grows and develops to meet the new challenges that technology and the demands of the marketplace put before it. Larry and his staff are now working on the next layer of the system, a project-control system that will enable them to automate the tasks of document management so that they don't have to rely only on people's professionalism alone to see each project through. They can build such a system because they have built the foundation of a rich data structure that can be understood and processed by the computer as well as by people.

One thing that they won't have to build, because they have had it from the start, is the commitment of the people. Far from being alienated by the introduction of this system, they gained a new feeling of control over the information. "There is an immediacy, a just-in-time factor when you tell people that content is going to be updated constantly," Vane says. "All the data is always ready; it has given a sense of urgency to the editorial process."

He remembers coming in on a Saturday to find one of the editors hard at work on the article about the space program. The space shuttle had linked up to the Russian Mir space station that morning. That evening was the deadline for the monthly updates to the CompuServe edition of the *Academic American Encyclopedia*. In the old days, it would have been the better part of a year before that story could have been in a published edition. But on this Saturday afternoon, this editor wasn't going to miss his chance to get that change in.

You can't build computer systems that have that kind of dedication. Computers, after all, are just machines. But if you have a staff with that kind of dedication, you can build a computer system that supports them. And you should!

CHAPTER 4

Sybase, Incorporated

The options for distributing information will get cheaper, easier, and allow for even faster updates. Today we publish on CD-ROM and we are testing delivery using the Web. Two or three years from now, there may be an even better distribution medium. But with our data in SGML, Sybase will be ready to take advantage of it.

—Steve Goodman, Director, Information Products Group, Sybase, Inc.

EXECUTIVE SUMMARY

THE GROUP
Information Products Group.

THEIR MISSION
Deliver Sybase's extensive library of technical product documentation to customers on CD-ROM.

TYPE OF APPLICATION
Production-oriented electronic publishing system.

SUMMARY
Many companies give CD-ROM publishing a try, as a way to reduce paper-handling costs or to make huge volumes of literature easier to search for their customers. Many can't figure out how to make electronic publishing work in their organizations for a reasonable cost.

Sybase, Incorporated can show you one way to do it. With hundreds of manuals and hundreds of thousands of pages of technical documentation supporting their products, Sybase, a manufacturer of client/server computer software, had a major information-delivery problem to solve. They wanted to make their technical information more useful for their customers, and electronic publishing was the obvious choice. The challenge was to find a way to satisfy customer demands while still keeping the publishing operation economically viable.

Sybase shipped its first technical documents on CD in August of 1994, building their system on SGML. By the end of the year, Sybase had saved enough to pay for the entire project. In 1995, Sybase saw additional savings of $5 million, and it will see even larger savings in the years ahead — savings that translate into reduced cost of revenue.

Publishing information electronically can save money and shorten time-to-market if you make the process an integral part of your production system. This case study will help shorten the learning curve at your company.

THE SAGA OF SYBOOKS™:
SYBASE, INCORPORATED

If you have ever wondered why some people make such a fuss about CD-ROM publishing, think about it from this fellow's perspective.

We'll say that he is the manager of information technology for a large manufacturing company. In that role he oversees the purchase of lots of software. Computer software is typically licensed, not sold, and the licensing fee is charged on a per-user basis. For companies like his, "site licensing" provides a convenient alternative to purchasing thousands of individual copies of a program. One flat payment gives him unlimited rights to use the software anywhere in the organization.

Our manager has purchased a site license from Sybase, Incorporated. Sybase makes high-end computer software used to build companywide information systems. His company uses Sybase products to build systems that support core business processes — executive reporting systems, production scheduling tools, customer records access programs, and so on. A site license makes good business sense.

So he gets a call from shipping and receiving informing him that the order from Sybase has arrived and he says, "Great. Bring it on up." Twenty minutes later — just long enough for him to start wondering when the guy from the loading dock is going to show up — *several* guys from the loading dock show up, towing pallets loaded up with boxes. And they tell him that they're going back down for more! It turns out that there are 14 pallets in all. (This is not going to fit in his office.) But it isn't so much the number of pallets that shocks him, it is what they carry. Because they aren't chock-full of software. The software itself takes up a fraction of the total shipment. The pallets are chock-full of *paper* — the manuals that go with the software!

This is a man who is going to make a fuss about putting information on CD-ROM.

Episodes like this actually happened to Sybase. And it didn't take too many of them before Sybase's senior management said, "There has got to be a better way."

THE BUSINESS CHALLENGE

It is easy to see how Sybase got into this situation. Founded in 1984, Sybase has been successful in that part of the software market known as "client/server computing." In client/server computing, data is stored and managed on central computers called servers. Desktop computers — the clients — contact the server to get data and then perform work like calculating totals and averages or formatting graphs (see Figure 4–1). Unlike the centralized mainframes of the 1960s and '70s, where one large computer stored all the data and did all the processing, client/server systems efficiently divide work between computers. Sybase was one of the first to deliver products for this market. Today the company offers a large number of complementary products in five categories: server products, application development tools, interoperability products, system-management software, and interactive multimedia programs.

Sybase puts a lot of resources into keeping its users well-informed. The company adds roughly 70,000 new or updated pages each year.

Client/server computing can be very efficient because relatively resource-hungry functions like sorting, formatting, and graphing data are done on relatively inexpensive end-user computers. Client/server computing can also be very complex because, unlike the mainframe model, where one program on one computer did all the work, client/server systems depend on a number of independent software programs cooperating to accomplish their tasks. The more software programs, the more complexity. The more complexity, the more documentation you need to describe it.

A well-informed user has fewer problems working with a product. Sybase puts a lot of resources into keeping its users well informed. The company has over 100 writers in 12 different groups located in sites spread across North America. Over 300,000 pages of technical information are in print, and Sybase adds roughly 70,000 new or updated pages each year.

Keeping that many people busy providing thorough information is an expensive proposition. Sybase spends millions of dollars every

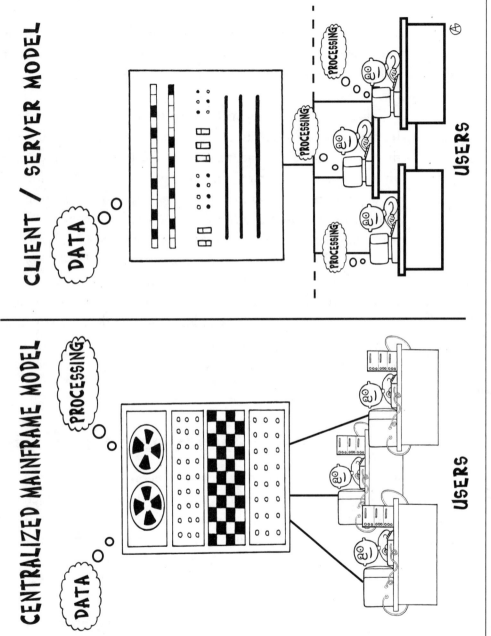

Figure 4–1. Client/server computing takes advantage of the processing power available on the end-user's desktop.

year to create technical documentation. Sybase was spending millions more to print, warehouse, and ship the books. The average set of manuals cost between $200 and $300 by the time it landed on an end-user's desk.

That is a lot of information for the user of the product to digest. It's the old needle-in-a-haystack problem — only here you have more than one haystack to search through. When products interact with one another, there is rarely just one place to look for information about a feature or a problem. For example, the documentation set for Sybase's Open Client/Server set of products consists of ten manuals with titles like *Open Client and Open Server Common Libraries Reference Manual, Client-Library/C Programmer's Guide, DB-library/C Reference Manual,* and *Tools and Connectivity Troubleshooting Guide.* Imagine being a programmer working on a new system for the top brass under a tight deadline and knowing that the answer you need to a vexing snag is somewhere in *that!* Your fondest dream is going to be some way of sifting through that print quickly to find the fact you need to know!

Reducing cost and enhancing usability of their product were two compelling reasons to make the shift to CD-ROM publishing.

A CORPORATE COMMITMENT TO STANDARDS

Technical documentation is not sold for a profit itself. It is part of the cost of the product. But it is a vital component of the product. Complex software is useless without it, and if users can't find the information they need in the manuals, direct customer-support costs — a far more expensive way to transmit knowledge — go way up. Reducing the cost and enhancing the usability of the product were two compelling reasons to make the shift to CD-ROM publishing.

CD-ROM publishing also made sense from a cultural perspective. Sybase has a corporate culture that says that you fix problems early in the process rather than later. You can see it in the way the company approaches quality initiatives.

Sybase was the first U.S. software company to achieve the highest level of ISO 9000/TickIT certification. ISO 9000 is an international quality standard established by the International Organization for Standardization (ISO).[1] TickIT is a subset of ISO 9000 which applies directly to the information-technology (IT) industry. ISO 9000 certification assures customers that a company has established basic quality systems in manufacturing and services. Certified companies are regularly audited to ensure that their standards are maintained; the certification is revoked if they are not. Becoming and staying ISO 9000 certified takes a significant corporate commitment of time, money, and management attention.

Sybase takes ISO 9000 very seriously. The company has invested well over $1 million in its ISO-9000-related activities, and the process is championed by senior executives throughout the company. The reason, in part, is that ISO 9000 provides a foundation for continuous improvement. The process of studying current manufacturing practices and developing standards and procedures gives the company means for monitoring and judging progress.

The same focus on quality and process demonstrated by its ISO 9000 certification affected the online publishing initiative. Sybase wasn't about to solve the information-delivery problem by giving its customers less information. The company was going to solve it by giving them the information in a form that would be easier to use.

---

1   The ISO is the international confederation of national standards bodies representing almost 100 countries. Based in Geneva, Switzerland, the ISO develops and distributes standards governing safety, quality, and uniformity for a wide variety of products and services. The United States representative to the ISO is the American National Standards Institute (ANSI). Another ISO standard is SGML. Officially it is ISO 8879:1986.

CHANGING THE WAY INFORMATION IS DELIVERED

The "14-pallet" episode crystallized everyone's thinking. If Sybase was to make technical information more accessible to its users and control its impact on product cost, they would have to make the switch from publishing on paper to publishing online. It was a strategic decision made at the senior management levels of the company. Tactical responsibility was assigned to the people who would have to live with the solution.

Denise Kiser, the director of information products, chaired an internal committee of publication managers to look for solutions and make recommendations. She gave the committee four goals:

1. Improve customer satisfaction by making documentation more accessible and easier to use.
2. Reduce the overall costs of publishing the information
3. Do it without increasing the postproduction time — the time from the moment the author finished the document to the time it was shipped to the customer
4. Do it in keeping with Sybase's reputation for technical innovation.

In 1994, Steve Goodman was a publications manager and a member of Denise's committee. He remembers all the ways they tried to figure out what their customers wanted from online documentation. "We commissioned a study of our users, talked to them at user-group meetings and trade shows, and took every opportunity to ask what would be important to them in online documentation."

Consistently, customers said that they wanted the documentation to be accurate and they wanted to be able to find the information they were looking for quickly. "Making the information more accessible was a major customer issue," Steve remembers. "Because the books tend to be large and exhaustive, and because material from several books might relate to what the programmer is trying to do, they wanted us to make it easier to find the right information in the right book."

A RAINBOW OF ONLINE PUBLISHING SOLUTIONS

There is no one single "right way" to publish information electronically. There is a broad range of possible solutions, each suitable for different types of business problems. Most companies pick whatever solution they can manage to produce with their word processing files. The solution may or may not be useful to their customers.

Sybase was looking specifically for a CD-based solution. Denise's committee kept looking until they found a solution that their customers liked. The possible solutions they looked at can be grouped into several broad categories:

1. **Send customers printable files.**

   PostScript is a page-printing language used by most high-end laser printers. With PostScript files, customers could print out the chapters they wanted to read.

   Sybase did, in fact, supply some of their customers with PostScript files on request. The committee later discovered that some of these customers were using programs to display the PostScript onscreen and read the documentation online. However, the idea of making that the Sybase solution was quickly jettisoned. The committee understood that their customers' problem was not just how to print or read manuals but also how to find information.

2. **Use the online viewer product made by the company that manufactured their desktop publishing program.**

This would have been the easiest solution. Many word processing and desktop publishing software manufacturers offer a viewer that will display their files onscreen. But when Sybase showed samples to customers, the solution was deemed too limited. It had limited capacity for searching or hypertext linking. Basically, it just projected print pages onto the screen. Print pages displayed onscreen turned out to be very awkward to read. Steve said, "We discovered that what works well for print doesn't work well online."

3. **Use a program that could search through files from different word processing or desktop publishing programs and display their contents onscreen.**

This solution looked promising on the surface. It had already been adopted by the customer service and support division to create AnswerBase™, a CD-ROM that gave customer support staff and customers access to all Sybase's technical bulletins and reference material right on their desktop systems.

This was a good solution for customer service, because their source materials came from a number of different sources in a number of different formats. AnswerBase enabled customer-support staff members to search this large collection of information quickly in order to find very specific answers.

However, the solution was not suitable for customers trying to learn to use a product or looking for general information. Its viewing capabilities were fairly limited, and it had little support for hypertext linking or other document-navigation features.

THE SOLUTION IS IN THE DATA

Early in 1994, Sybase looked at a number of different products that could be used to publish on CD-ROM, including one that used SGML for its data. Steve remembers that "The SGML tool was an immediate hit." Users responded positively to its familiar metaphors, including a dual-window display showing a table of contents on one side and the content on the other. Books were stored in collections, and the reader could search an entire collection as well as the individual books within it. Cross references in a book were hypertext links to the referenced material, and readers could create links of their own. They could annotate the book with private notes or with public notes that could be shared with other readers.

These features were not unique to the SGML prototype. Many online publishing tools could provide similar capabilities. But the SGML tool had other advantages as well. For one thing, it was available on all the different computer platforms that Sybase products ran on. More importantly, it would enable Sybase to modify the format used to display the information to suit those different computers without having to physically change the files for every computer platform. *That* Sybase took very seriously.

Most online publishing programs must have formatting instructions inserted directly into the text of a book in order to control how it is displayed. To change the way a book looks on the screen, you must go into the text and change the formatting codes. To change *all* the books on a CD, you have to change the formatting codes in every one of the books. In practice, this quickly becomes labor intensive and expensive.

The SGML product, in contrast, formatted books using structure-oriented display filters — specifications that described which element types should be displayed and how each element type should look

The SGML tool enabled Sybase to modify the display on different computers without having to physically change the files. That Sybase took very seriously.

onscreen. Using display filters, all of the books in a category — user manuals, reference manuals, etc. — could be formatted using the settings in one file. To change the way a set of books looked, you didn't have to touch the books themselves, you just changed the display filter. This was a far more efficient way to manage formatting for large volumes of documents (see Figure 4–2).

An aside: Most of today's word processing programs have features commonly referred to as "style sheets." Style sheets are fundamentally different from the display filters just described. Word processing style sheets — also called "templates" — are simply a convenient way to quickly apply one or more formatting commands to pieces of text. To change the way a document is displayed, you still have to change the document itself. Word processing style sheets don't support the kind of separation between a document's content and how it is displayed that is fundamental to SGML.

Sybase would later discover that display filters offered advantages they had not originally considered. For example, they could produce customized documents by applying different display filters to an existing set of manuals — without having to create a new copy of the documents. Sybase publishes short summaries of programming commands called "Quick Reference Guides." Steve discovered that they could produce the guides simply by writing a new filter for the manuals. The display filter hid all the content that was not part of a command summary.

"We were drawn to the good presentation of the SGML-based prototype," Steve recalls. "What wasn't immediately obvious to us was that it was the underlying structure of the SGML data that made those presentation capabilities possible."

SGML addressed their production and delivery issues and gave them data in a vendor-independent format. They would not find themselves locked into one solution or one vendor down the road because the cost of getting data out of that vendor's system and into a new one was prohibitive. "SGML," Steve says, "was the only logical solution."

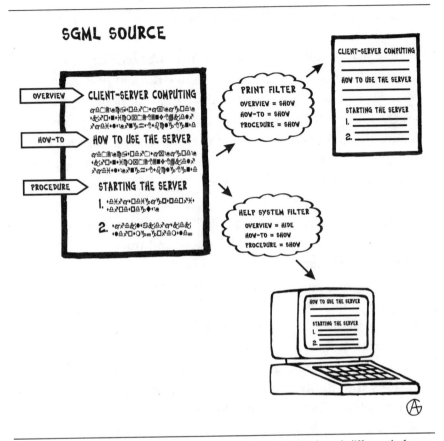

Figure 4–2. SGML data can be processed so that it is displayed differently for different uses.

BUILDING A NEW SYSTEM

Based on customer reactions and the other advantages that SGML offered, the committee selected the SGML solution. In March of 1994, Steve joined Denise's organization and took charge of implementing the project.

Steve would need to do more than just convert existing manuals to SGML; this was not a one-shot project. Sybase documentation is constantly changing to reflect developments to their products. Steve had to make SGML and CD-ROM publishing an everyday part of the writers' jobs.

How that would be done was less than obvious. Up to this time, writers had understood their job to be to write and produce finished pages. As long as the pages looked good in print, nobody gave much thought to what the writers did in their word processing software to produce them. As a consequence, Sybase discovered what every company discovers when it switches to electronic publishing — that the documents they were producing every day were not good raw material for an online publishing system.

They were not good raw material because the formatting in their files varied from document to document and from writer to writer, sometimes significantly. "Corporate standards were in place," Steve says, "but writers still focused on the printout. Those who were most focused on print tended to take liberties with the standards to get the effect they wanted." That unpredictable formatting made it impossible to write software with 100% guaranteed accuracy that would automatically convert from the format used to print the file to the format used to display it online. The programmer of the conversion program would have to account for every possible formatting variation that any writer could ever create. What Sybase's technical writers would need was a system that helped them stick to the corporate standards as they wrote.

Yet it would be impossible to stop ongoing work while they completely retooled their system. So they decided to move the project forward in two phases. Phase I would get a core body of their most widely read documents converted to SGML and delivered on CD-ROM to customers. It would "seed the field" by introducing customers to the online documentation early and by getting the SGML tool installed on their systems. Phase II would address the more challenging problem of the writing environment.

STEP ONE: SEED THE FIELD

The objectives for Phase I were to get the SGML reader software out to a broad base of their customers and to build a preliminary version of the desktop-publishing-to-SGML conversion system. Their strategy was simple. "We planned to mass-ship a CD with our most popular titles to all our customers," Steve says. "That way, we ensured that our users would be encouraged to install the CD, and we could start to see savings right away by scaling back the costs of the print editions." Sybase also ensured that subsequent CDs would deliver documentation updates to an audience prepared to receive them.

Sybase brought in Passage Systems, as their outside consultants, to help them implement the project. Bob Glushko, VP and chief scientist for Passage, recalls that Sybase undertook the project at an opportune time. "Sybase was smart — they didn't attempt to cut over to the new online environment while they were doing a major product release. They did it at an interim release, when the books weren't changing dramatically. That made it easier to manage the conversion to SGML."

Converting that first set of documents to SGML was handled by Passage. They already had plenty of experience dealing with word processing and desktop publishing files that had writing irregularities in them. Although this would be too costly and time-consuming a way to produce SGML on an ongoing basis, it was the best way to get a critical mass of documents converted to SGML without disrupting the projects that were actively underway at Sybase.

Meanwhile, Steve's team wrote the programs to install the product on a wide set of computer platforms. They also worked iteratively with Passage to define and refine the new SGML environment. This activity focused particularly on analyzing their documents, modifying the word processor templates they used, and designing the display filters that would control the online display. Their goal was to have one CD that would run on any computer that ran Sybase products. That's not as easy as it sounds. To do it, they had to support ten flavors of the UNIX operating system (HP. HP-UX 9.0, IBM AIX 3.2, AT&T 3000, SGI IRIX 5.2.x, Sun SunOS 4.1.x OpenWin, Sun SunOS 4.1.x Motif, Sun Solaris 2.x OpenWin, Sun Solaris 2.x Motif, Novell UnixWare 1.1, DEC OSF/1), three different versions of Windows (3.1, 95, and NT), IBM's OS/2, and the Apple Macintosh. (Even then, there were still a few platforms that the CD would not run on.)

Because of the volume of CDs they would be shipping, the installation and configuration process had to be bulletproof. Because the CDs would be given with the product at no extra cost, support costs had to be kept negligible. "Installation issues can be a real headache for the tech-support people," Steve explains. "Industrywide, install problems are typically about 30% of the total calls to tech support. Now we go and ship a new CD to *all* our customers. You can imagine how popular we would be with tech support if one-third of those customers started calling the hot line with install problems."

GETTING THE WORD PROCESSOR UNDER CONTROL

While Passage was converting existing files to SGML, they were also creating revised word processor style sheets that closely matched the SGML document structure. When writers used the style sheets, and didn't deviate from them, their files would convert directly to SGML.

Sybase and Passage worked together to develop the style sheets. Steve explains that "This type of development is by its nature iterative. It required a lot of knowledge about how the writers were using the existing templates. Passage could handle the SGML syntax, but they couldn't be expected to absorb all that goes into such a large body of documentation as quickly as the schedule called for." In fact, work on the style sheets continued even after the first CD was shipped.

When the new style sheets were ready, Passage brought the first collection of files into conformance with them. Bob describes this process as "author amnesty." He explains: "Too often, people look at the inconsistent formatting in the old files like the writer did something wrong. But you have to realize that it wasn't a crime at the time. *Then* the focus was on producing camera-ready copy. *Now* the focus is on something more rigorous. It is demotivating to make writers stop writing and reformat all their files. So we tweaked the templates and we brought the first files into line with those templates ourselves."

Remember that these were the most widely read documents that Sybase published. Bringing them into alignment with the new standard made sense for several reasons. First, it quickly brought a big chunk of Sybase's corporate intelligence about its products up to a new quality standard. Second, the writers could keep working productively on new information.

A NEW PRODUCT: SYBOOKS — INTERACTIVE DOCUMENTATION FOR SYBASE PRODUCTS

Phase I was successfully completed in August 1994, when Sybase shipped its first CD, under the name SyBooks, to 13,000 customers. By December, they had saved nearly a million dollars in reduced printing costs — more than enough money to repay the cost of the project, including additional staff, consulting fees, the licensing fees for the SGML online publishing software, new equipment, and the cost of the free CD to every customer.

Moreover, they averaged only six technical-support cases per month, an error rate of less than 0.01%. And the positive feedback they received really gave them a boost as they went to work on Phase II.

STEP TWO: BUILD THE ENVIRONMENT

In late 1994, Phase II began the larger job of creating a production environment that would enable writers to create SGML internally. Steve's challenge was to change a publications environment that was geared toward producing paper to one geared to generating SGML.

He had three key requirements:

1. **Sybase's writers would keep the word processor they were already using.**

   Although a number of writing tools on the market are specifically geared toward producing SGML, the technical writing teams were satisfied with the desktop publishing tool they already had. It gave them a very complete set of features, more than were available with SGML authoring tools at the time. And it represented a significant corporate investment in training, expertise, and system infrastructure, not to mention in their existing files. "We had a pretty tight system already," Steve says. "We didn't see why we should have to scrap the whole thing just because we were going to output SGML."

2. **They would be able to preview the online version of a book at any time.**

   One key to making the new environment work was to get writers to think about preparing material for online delivery while they were writing, not after the writing was finished. So a system was needed that would let them preview what the online version of the book was going to look like at any time.

   The system would also need tools that checked for errors and gave the writer useful feedback when errors were discovered.

3. **The writers would not have to learn SGML.**

> A core premise of SGML is that documents have structure, organization, and logic. The writers already needed to concentrate on those aspects of documents. They should not have to know the particulars of SGML itself any more than they had to know PostScript in order to use their printers.

The key to success in Phase II was to get the writers to switch gears, not switch products. Bob Glushko concurs with Steve's goals. "I believe that consistently formatted documents and a good filter, supported by good document debugging, is a powerful model for many organizations."

UNDERSTANDING AND SUPPORTING WRITERS' ISSUES

The focus on print output is a hard one for writers to give up. Few people adjust easily to sudden change, no matter how smooth or well organized. "It's ironic," Steve says, "but considering that they write about technology, writers can be a bit shy about changing the technology they write with." To help them through the transition, Steve set up the Writers' Tools Group, a three-person support team to help writers troubleshoot problems, provide training and consulting to writing groups, maintain the publishing environment, and enhance the SyBooks display filters.

A dedicated help desk contributed toward building a core of expertise in the early stages of Phase II that would prove useful as the new system was extended to more and more writing groups throughout the company. The Writers' Tools Group quickly learned what was working and what wasn't. As they found adjustments that were needed to the corporate standards, or common mistakes that writers kept making, they incorporated that information into process improvements.

The SyBooks development team also built utilities — small programs to accomplish specific, targeted functions — that eased the transition burden for the writers and increased their productivity. "For example, we developed a utility that we called 'Fix Legacy,'" Steve remembers. "It helped writers take existing word processor files and convert them to the new template." Programs like this one made a big difference in the writers' ability to get up to speed on the new system and to automate tasks that they had previously done by hand. In fact, most of the utilities were done in response to needs that the writers fingered. In the past, they had not thought about automating their chores, because there is very little automated processing that you can reliably do with word processing files. "There's so much you can do to process SGML data," Steve says, "as opposed to the older system where there was very *little* you could do."

> "There's so much you can do to process SGML data, as opposed to the older system where there was very little you could do."
>
> —Steve Goodman

THE NEW SYSTEM

The new system first went live at corporate headquarters in Emeryville, CA. Since then, SyBooks systems have been deployed to Sybase offices in Mountain View, CA, Burlington, MA, and Boulder, CO. The SyBooks system tied the word processor the writers were already using into an end-to-end process that gave them "continuous production."

In the traditional publishing model, production is a separate step that starts after the writing is over. If there is a problem with the files, it can throw the whole schedule off. With their new system, Sybase has an environment where writing and production have been brought together. A writer can see, at any stage in the process, whether the document he or she is writing complies with the template and how it will look online (see Figure 4–3).

"That's the key concept," Bob Glushko says. "'Continuous production' is the secret to controlling the process. Instead of WYSIWYG — 'What You See Is What You Get' — the writers now have

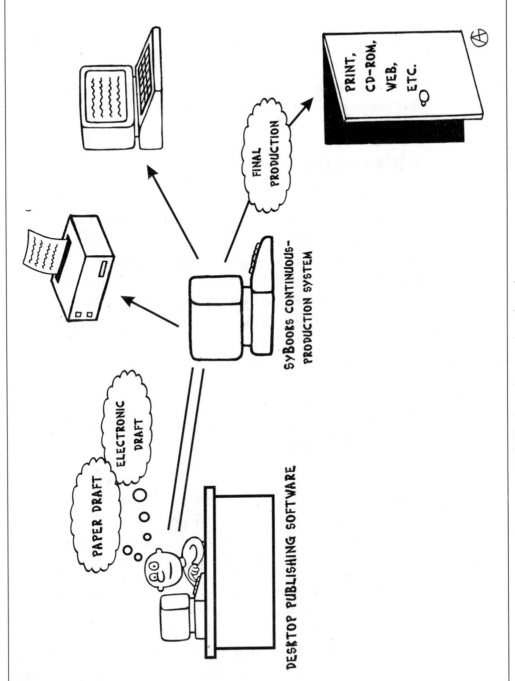

Figure 4–3. Sybase's system lets writers see the finished product anytime they choose.

WYSIWCG — 'What You See Is What the Customer Gets.' It gives writers the satisfaction of seeing their end product, without having to be concerned that they are producing valid SGML behind the scenes."

THE PAYOFFS

In the end, Sybase didn't *just* deliver books on a CD-ROM. That's the first tangible deliverable, but behind it is a new approach to managing and publishing information that Steve describes as "opening up a whole new universe of applications for our information." "When we look back five years from now," he says, "the applications that are now possible — document management, interactive manuals, expert systems — may supersede online documentation as the primary payoff from using SGML."

Even at this early stage, Sybase can point to the following tangible benefits:

Four months after they shipped their first CD, Sybase had saved enough in reduced materials costs alone to pay for the entire project.

- **Sybase has realized major reductions in the cost of its products with SyBooks.**

  By December 1994, four months after they shipped their first CD, Sybase had saved enough in reduced materials costs alone to pay for the entire project: the new staff, consulting costs, software licensing fees and equipment purchases, as well as the cost of producing and shipping that first free CD to every customer.

  These savings grow dramatically as Sybase brings more collections of technical documentation into SyBooks. Sybase saw savings of approximately $5 million for 1995, the first full year with SyBooks in production. Steve notes that these were just the savings in material costs. They don't include savings in warehousing and shipping.

The recent release of the Sybase System 11™ product line, the first major release of their flagship client/server products since the SyBooks project began, was a major opportunity for SyBooks and the new information-publishing environment to show what it could do. "We were able to deliver books in both electronic form and paper without adding time to our production cycle," Steve says. "In fact, now that we are also delivering documentation using the World Wide Web, we have shortened the cycle significantly. We can make manuals available to our users within a few days of their leaving the writers' hands." (See the discussion of the Web below.)

- **SyBooks has satisfied its customers.**

   Steve says this is "far and away the number-one benefit." Not all Sybase technical documents are available yet as SyBooks. But for those that are, less than 2% of their customers choose to order the paper versions. The majority are sticking with SyBooks.

   Sybase has an active international user's group. At a recent user-group convention, SyBooks and online documentation in general were hot topics. Two conclusions emerged from the debate: the conference attendees wanted a uniform interface to any and all electronic information offered by Sybase. And they preferred SyBooks over the non-SGML interfaces currently being provided by Sybase.

- **Sybase can put its technical documentation out over the World Wide Web — for a marginal added cost.**

   If CDs shorten the cycle for delivering updated information to a few weeks, the Internet's World Wide Web offers the possibility of shortening it to almost nothing! Instead of copying and sending a disk to every customer, you need only put the documents on your Web site and then tell everyone where to find them.

However, most companies looking into the Web face an unpalatable choice between paying to reformat existing text into HyperText Markup Language (HTML) or waiting for their product vendors to give them a tool that will translate their word processing files for them. Either way, there's both an extra expense and added production time to take advantage of this new distribution channel.

Sybase began the SyBooks project before the Web took off as a popular way to distribute technical information. But once they decided that it was a viable option, they didn't have to face those choices. Because they had their information in SGML, all they needed to do to make it available on the Web was write a new display filter (another unanticipated benefit of those display filters!). "Getting books up on the Web," Steve says, "was incredibly easy" (see Figure 4–4).

Steve envisions CDs as an interim step on the way to distributed information publishing, probably over the Internet. "Distribution will get even cheaper, easier, and it will allow for even faster updates," he says. "Two or three years from now, there may be an even better distribution medium than the Internet. But with our data in SGML, we will be ready to take advantage of it."

- **Sybase is reducing translation costs.**

Sybase is beginning to realize cost savings in other areas. One of the first is in foreign-language translation.

To this day, translation remains as much an art as a science. Sophisticated (and expensive!) autotranslation programs can sometimes speed the process, depending on the quality of the original writing, but native speakers must still review the entire document for accuracy.

What *is* surprising is that translation costs are no less expensive the second time around! For word processing files, there are no reliable, automatic tools that can find only those parts of a document that have changed since the last edition. Translating a new edition of a manual remains a very — well, manual — task.

Sybase's Japanese contractors are now switching to SGML. They will be able to use standard utility programs to highlight the differences between the previous and current SGML versions of a document and pinpoint only those parts of the content that have changed. Steve expects that they can write a utility to automatically move the revised English portion of the new edition into the original translated document at the right location so that the

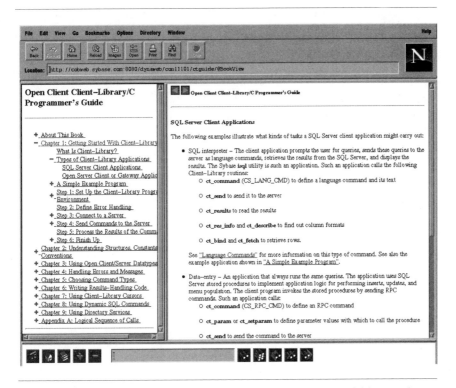

Figure 4–4. With SGML, Sybase made its CD-ROM documents available over the World Wide Web in record time. *Courtesy of Sybase, Inc.*

translators can retranslate that section in place. Steve says, "Our translation costs are going to drop quite a bit."

Steve cautions that SGML is not always easy. "It helps when embarking on a project like this to work with a company that knows the field well," he says. Even after the initial development, work has continued on the SyBooks system. In Sybase's case, the dependencies between the writing templates, conversion routines, and SGML display filters means that they will have ongoing maintenance expenses for some time. (Fortunately, developers of SGML systems have recognized these same problems, and new, more flexible tools are coming out all the time.)

But Steve also believes that the effort is worthwhile. "We've really just begun to jump into this," he says. "But we have already seen the benefits. With the improvement we've seen in productivity, we can focus more of our development time on giving people better information about the Sybase products." Better use of resources, reusable information, vendor independence, and satisfied customers — looks like Sybase is onto a very good thing.

CHAPTER 5

United Technologies
Sikorsky Aircraft
Corporation

*The challenges for all businesses in the 1990s
are the same: do more with less, and do it better.*

— Richard Weich, Director of Technical Support Services

EXECUTIVE SUMMARY

THE GROUP

Customer Service, Technical Support Services Branch.

THEIR MISSION

Produce the technical publications, training information, and logistics data for Sikorsky Helicopters.

TYPE OF APPLICATION

Collaborative writing and automated document-production environment.

SUMMARY

In 1987, whenever they won another helicopter contract, Sikorsky Aircraft had to hire another group of technical writers. The writing and publishing system they used made it impossible to reuse material that had already been written, with the result that every contract's set of supporting documentation cost between $3 and $5 million — even if the content was virtually the same as a set that already existed.

In 1995, having reengineered their system using SGML, Sikorsky produced 60% more material with fewer than half the original staff, and its end product is noticeably more accurate and more consistent. The cost of documenting each new version of a helicopter is incremental and directly related to the volume of changes required. The time required for production has been significantly reduced as well. Best of all, storing the data in SGML lets Sikorsky produce electronic products such as Interactive Electronic Technical Manuals (IETM), computer-based training packages and expert system diagnostics automatically, at a negligible cost. Sikorsky sees this as a competitive advantage in the growing civilian marketplace.

The problems Sikorsky identified and solved are problems still faced by many companies today, despite the widespread use of word processing and computer-aided drafting programs. But where Sikorsky had to build its system largely from scratch, companies today have a much larger pool of products to choose from. For Sikorsky, SGML was a major undertaking; today, SGML is just common sense.

If any single case study shows how corporations can meet this challenge using SGML, that case study is Sikorsky Aircraft Corporation, a United Technology Company. Sound like a success you might like to replicate in your organization? Then read on.

BUILDING BLOCKS TO BETTER INFORMATION: SIKORSKY AIRCRAFT CORPORATION

A helicopter is not a simple device. It takes a lot of supporting information — maintenance procedures, troubleshooting tests, training materials, and so on — in order for people to use it properly and take care of it. Of course, the same can be said for more and more of today's advanced-technology products. Whether it is an aircraft, an automobile, or an air conditioner, each new model just becomes more complex to own, operate, and service.

Helicopters, however, have an additional wrinkle that your average under-the-counter coffee makers or vacuum cleaners don't have. If not used or maintained properly, they can experience mishaps that we'd just as soon avoid. Owners, users, and governments all take a dim view of this happening, so over the years the requirements for supporting helicopters with thorough documentation have grown substantially. Industry groups such as the Air Transport Association and government oversight agencies such as the FAA have invested a lot of time and money in standardizing the requirements for documentation so that nothing falls through the cracks. This thoroughness is why most of us wouldn't think twice about jumping aboard a chopper, but it also adds up to a lot of paper, typically 18 to 20 thousand pages for a single aircraft.

In 1987, Sikorsky Aircraft — like most other aircraft manufacturers in the world — created that paper by hand. (And if you are amazed to discover that companies were still assembling pages by hand in 1987, then hold onto your hat! There are plenty of companies still doing it that way today!)

As you can imagine, this took a lot of work. Here is how a typical book got done.

TWELVE WEEKS IN THE LIFE
OF A TYPICAL PROJECT

It would all start with the technical writer. When a helicopter needed a manual, a writer was assigned to the project. The new manual was usually based on one that already existed, so the writer would start editing a copy of the existing manual by hand. When he was ready to review a draft of the manual, he sent it through the page-layout process.

The first step in laying out pages was to typeset the text. A trained operator would retype the writer's material on a typesetting machine, adding long, cryptic strings of characters that controlled the look of the finished text. The result was page after page of words rendered in the proper typeface and weight for the final book. (The typesetter's file was useless to the writer, by the way, because of all those extra control characters stuck into the text. When the writer later needed another change, the process had to be done all over again.) While the typesetter was formatting the text, graphic artists were creating the drawings and graphics needed for the book.

Once the text and the graphics were prepared, a layout artist took the typeset pages of text, cut them into blocks of text, and pasted the blocks down one by one onto heavy paper boards. Each board would become one page of the manual. The artist also pasted on the headers and footers at the top and bottom of each page and, of course, the illustrations.

Only now, with the final pages finished, could the writer assemble the table of contents and the index. Those pages had to go through typesetting and layout themselves, of course, after which the writer had a finished draft of the book which could be sent around for review.

Sound expensive and slow? It was both. Labor costs for the production effort alone ran about $2.25 per page. They scrapped 50% of the first round of pages and 25% of the second, so there were thousands of dollars of rework on every project. And it took an average of twelve weeks to turn the pages around. Any requests for changes from the engineers simply couldn't be accommodated if they came in during the last few weeks before the publication needed to be shipped.

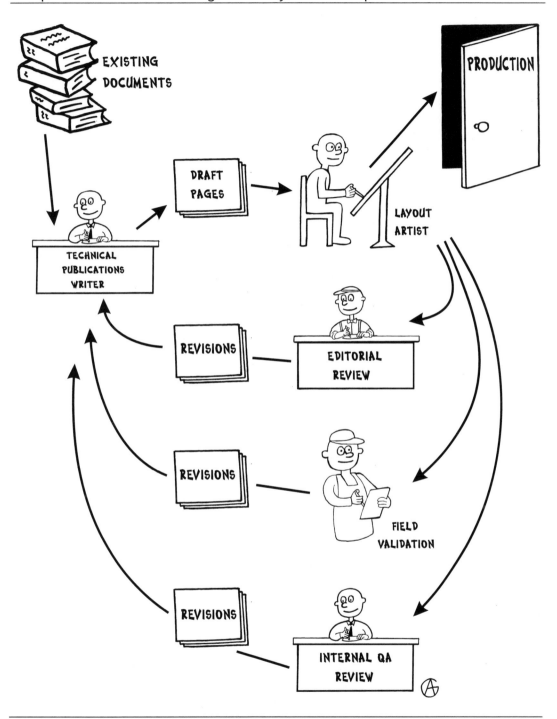

Figure 5–1. Helicopter documentation usually took 18 months to go through production and reach the field.

LOOKING FOR SOLUTIONS
IN ALL THE WRONG PLACES

Everyone knew that the costs of publishing all this support information was spiraling out of control. Customers were starting to say, "Hey, I could buy another helicopter for that money!" It was clear that the effort required to create all this product data and then keep it up to date was increasing exponentially. It was clear that the quality, the accuracy, and the consistency of the information was suffering.

What wasn't clear was what to do to fix it.

Sikorsky had undertaken initiatives that looked promising, but the initiatives had not resulted in big payoffs in either productivity or cost savings. They had installed a Wang word processing system in 1985. Writers were not taking to it because it didn't result in any benefit for them. For most projects, it was faster for the writers to make hand edits to a printed copy of the book and send that over to the typesetters than it was to retype the manuals on the new system. And even if they did type text in the word processor, the typesetter still had to reformat the file with typesetting codes, and, from that point on, edits were made to the printed version.

Sikorsky also investigated replacing typesetting with a page-layout system. They found it would give them at most a 5% return on the investment. That was hardly the scale of improvement they needed.

In 1987, Richard Weich was put in charge of the technical support services, with the charge to solve this problem. His supervisor said, "You need to improve the level of automation." But neither of them knew what that meant.

Rich is quick to point out that he considers himself a computer illiterate. "If I had come from a publishing background," he says, "or if I had been more familiar with computers, I think it would have been harder for me to find a solution to this problem. I would have already had preconceived notions about how it should be done."

But Rich did know the company's product inside and out, and he did know what the customers needed in the way of support materials.

Rich's background at Sikorsky included front-line customer-service experience, and he was working as a customer support manager for international contracts in the mid-1980s. So early on, he had experience with the information needs of the international customers.

FUNDAMENTAL PROBLEMS WITH THE PROCESS

Rich began looking at how the work actually got done. He followed the trail of information as it moved through the department. And he quickly became convinced that, if the business challenges were cost, capacity, and quality, they were a direct result of three process problems.

- **Problem Number 1: Writers were rewriting the same text over and over again.**

    Sounds like this problem should have been obvious and easy to solve. But at the time nobody had any idea how to build a writing system that would let authors share common text, so nobody thought of this as a "process problem." This was just how things were done. What people today are calling "collaborative writing environments" didn't even exist back then. Weren't even a gleam in anybody's eye. The most sophisticated notion anyone had for collaborative writing was, "I'll give you a copy of my file."

    But when Rich and his team looked at the documents themselves, they found that much of the text was the same — in some cases, as much as 80%. For example, one helicopter contract might specify that the radio be installed to the pilot's right, while another contract specified that it be installed on the pilot's left. The radio itself was the same. Nevertheless, writers were rewriting the entire radio section from scratch for each contract.

    This didn't make any sense. "Even if the customer wanted the same exact model as another contract, and the only thing we had to change was the model number," Rich observed; " it still cost $3 to $5 million to produce the doc set."

> *"Even if the customer wanted the same exact model and the only thing we had to change was the model number, it would still cost $3 to 5 million to produce the doc set."*
>
> —Richard Weich

Clearly, one solution they needed was a way for writers to share the common content and only have to write about what was different.

- **Problem Number 2: Writing was going on in three different departments with three different missions, yet each was writing lots of the same stuff over and over again.**

Sikorsky had three different groups writing technical information:

1. Technical Publications
2. Training
3. Logistics Support Analysis (LSA)

Each of these groups had come into existence at a different time to solve a different problem, and each reported to a different part of Sikorsky's management. When Rich came to the technical support services department in 1987, both the technical publications and training groups were brought into his department. It was the first time any of these groups had reported to the same management.

It immediately became clear that each group was doing some of the others' work. Rich realized that "each group independently researched, authored, and updated support data for air vehicle systems . . . . To one degree or another, each group was producing the same information independently."

The reasons they were doing overlapping work were simple:

1. Each group had evolved as a separate operation with a unique business mission.
2. Each group was in a different location and reported to a different manager.
3. Each group had systems and processes that they had developed on their own to get their work done. The systems were not compatible.

4. The groups could not share common information, so when one group needed something that another group may have already created, they had to rewrite it for themselves.

5. Each had different customer delivery dates and different counterparts on the customer side.

All this added up to a situation where the pressures worked to keep them focused on maintaining their separate identities instead of pooling their talents and resources. The solution was going to have to enable each of these groups to focus on their area of expertise and eliminate the overlapping efforts.

■ **Problem Number 3: The production process for the finished manuals was still slow and labor intensive.**

As we saw earlier, the work involved in producing a manual was expensive and tedious. They were not manufacturing information; they were hand-crafting it! The process was so slow that, in many cases, it took 18 months for a manual to move from the writer's desk to the field technicians who needed it.

Rich realized that the solution would involve more than just bringing in a new computer system. It would involve process and organizational changes as well. And none of it would be possible unless they could find a technology that would support sharing the common content across books and teams.

GETTING THE SPIN ON THE RIGHT SOLUTION

Up until now, everybody had been so busy getting the current jobs done that nobody could sit back and ask what the right solution would look like. "While we were arguing about the causes of the problems — who was at fault, which groups had the most difficult job, etc. — we realized that we had lost sight of our mission: to provide quality logistics information to our customers. We also realized we could solve the problems . . . by focusing on the creation and management of recyclable information."

Sounds right; but how do you do that? Rich decided this was a question that the people producing the information — the writers, artists, production staff — had to answer themselves.

"Around the end of '87, when we started to get out from under our backlog and see the light of day, I had each group in the department elect a representative to a task force. Then I gave them three instructions: (1) To look at the problems they were encountering today and describe their ideal world — the tools, processes, and so on that would solve their problems. (2) Think about what they would need five years down the road. Solve the problems of producing not only today's product, but also the products they would need to offer in the future. (3) Don't read any magazines, don't go to any shows, and don't talk to any vendors. I was convinced that would just confuse everybody."

Rich divided the task force into two groups, one for graphics and one for publishing. Joe Salerno, his computer-systems administrator, would coordinate their activities and write the requests for proposals.

With this charge, the teams went to work. Wild-guess time: for which team did things go easiest? Answer: the graphics team. They came back with a 30-page requirements document that Joe turned into a Request for Proposal. It was circulated to vendors in 1988, and installation of a system began in 1989. What most people assumed would be the hard part — the graphics — had gone smoothly, so the prognosis looked good for the text side.

But text is harder to work with than you would think. Joe Salerno worked with the members of the publishing task force to boil their wish list down into a requirements spec. The process took over a month. It turned out that, once writers and editors started to think about what they would *really* need in order to streamline their primary task — producing manuals — everybody could think of lots and lots of problems that would have to be solved. It took a year to turn the research and interviews into the RFP. When they were all done, the spec was over 100 pages long — without all the supporting exhibits and sample pages! Then they let it out to the vendors.

Because the specification was so complex, Rich decided to hold a bidders conference. In April of 1989, representatives from ten of the leading companies in the text processing and publishing field gathered at Sikorsky to review the requirements.

"And the response we got from all the vendors . . . well, they told us we were insane." The bidders told them that Sikorsky's fundamental requirements — modular text components that would be reused automatically in every doc that they belonged to, automatic composition of technical manuals out of the database, and so on — could not be done by any computer program in existence.

Joe remembers that "There wasn't much vision from the publishing vendors back then." For example, the spec described a system for automatically linking one section of a document to another, so that if a later change affected the pagination of the rest of the document, the tables of contents, indexes, and the cross references would not have to be redone. Today we call that "hypertext." Back then, the vendors said; "There's no way to do that!" Another example; the spec described merging the pictures and diagrams directly into the text. Commonplace today. The vendors didn't have any idea how to do it.

Rich responded, "This is a solution that makes sense. You are all smart folks; I'm sure you'll come up with something."

The RFP was so precise and so technically demanding that several vendors choose not to bid on the contract at all. Eventually, six vendors came back with proposals, and the process of choosing a supplier began.

SELLING IT UPSTAIRS

In the computer business, "shrink wrapped" refers to a computer program that you can use right out of the box. Just unwrap it, install it, and go to work; no customizing required. "Shrink wrapped" is what everybody wants. But to Rich's team, it was obvious from the start that the solution to their problem would be neither shrink wrapped nor inexpensive.

Rich also knew that top management's approval for an appropriation of this magnitude would not be automatic. The company had already made a big investment in the Wang WP system, and he was going to have to explain why that solution wasn't working and never would.

Another subtle issue had to be addressed as well. Managers were not sufficiently familiar with the process of producing documentation to recognize why shrink-wrapped solutions could not work. "Our business is making helicopters, so helicopters are what everyone thinks about," Rich observed. "People understood spending money on equipment to support manufacturing. But they didn't instinctively identify training and publications as key parts of the product that had to be manufactured as well."

People understand spending money on equipment to support manufacturing. But they don't instinctively identify training and publications as key parts of the product that have to be manufactured as well.

Fortunately, Sikorsky management did have a history of paying attention to data-management and manufacturing-automation issues. In the 1960s, Sikorsky had been one of the first aerospace companies to invest in computer-aided-design (CAD) systems. By the 1980s, teams like the engineering automation group were at work developing systems for Sikorsky's computer-integrated-manufacturing (CIM) environment. If Rich had to do some educating, he was speaking to an audience willing to learn.

In order to explain the vision to senior management, Rich prepared a briefing about the need to automate the technical-publications and training process. Over the next 18 months, he would give the presentation more than 30 times to every level of corporate management.

The presentation focused on the documentation process: how it worked at that time and how it would work when automated. (In fact, the diagrams in this chapter are based on Rich's presentation.) In a series of diagrams, the audience was walked through the production steps a typical project followed, from the writer's first draft, through cycles of cut-and-paste composition, engineering review and field testing, the physical publishing process itself, and finally to the aircraft technician —

18 months later! For many in his audience, it was their first glimpse at how labor intensive and slow the technical publishing process remained, even in the midst of radical changes to Sikorsky's design and engineering operations.

In the second set of slides, Rich showed how the process could work if it were intelligently automated (see Figure 5-2). The individual pieces of paper and isolated process arrows from the first diagram were replaced by a central database, a repository for engineering diagrams, logistical support data, vendor information, graphics, and text. All the parties involved in the development and approval of a document had access to the database, so they could see real-time versions of the manual on demand. Engineering and QA review could take place electronically, not be held up by another round of manual page composition. Instead of pasting up reproducible copy page by page and sending it to the printer to be printed, Sikorsky could deliver electronic files straight to the printer, which they in turn converted directly into the plates that went on the big printing presses. The opportunity for time and cost savings was impressive.

Rich also pointed out the forces driving these changes. One key force was the Department of Defense's CALS initiative, a mandate that all defense contractors supply their information in SGML and other open standards in the future.[1] Sikorsky could certainly expect this to affect their business.

---

1   CALS is the United States Department of Defense's project to develop data standards for the product information it receives from its vendors. CALS relies heavily on the use of international standards, including SGML. Although the CALS acronym has been used consistently from the beginning, it has had several different meanings. It currently stands for *Commerce At Light Speed*, a distinctly more marketing-oriented interpretation than the previous *Continuous Acquisition and Lifecycle Support.*

Today, SGML permeates the airline industry. The Air Transport Association's (ATA) Specification 100 is the SGML standard for technical information used in ground support and maintenance of commercial aircraft. Many companies in commercial aviation today — including the likes of Boeing, McDonnell-Douglas, United, and USAir — use the ATA 100 to streamline the development and management of enormous volumes of information. Sikorsky came early to the realizations that the rest of the industry has since followed.

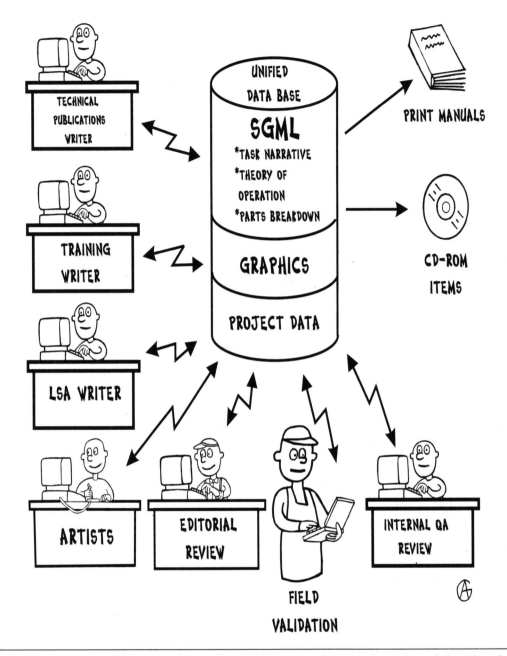

Figure 5–2. Online access to current content, graphics, and project data has substantially reduced turnaround time.

The senior managers at Sikorsky signed off on the appropriation — but not before they put one restriction on the project: Rich would have to deliver reports on the payback and payoff every quarter. Though payback was originally slated to take five years to achieve, Rich was able to file his last report in year three because "the savings were so good."

PICKING THE SOLUTION

From the six original submissions, Rich's team whittled the contenders down to three who came the closest to the requirements on paper. Then they invited them in for two-week benchmarking trials on site.

The trials were more like ordeals, for the team and the vendors both. At the end of each day, the team would get together and share the results of the day's events with the members of the vendor's team. The vendor could come back the next day with a proposed fix. The trials ended up running seven days a week, 12 hours or more each day, as the vendor teams went back to their hotel rooms and worked until 2 or 3 a.m. trying to deal with the problems they encountered.

By the end of the trials, Rich realized that *nobody* could deliver a system that handled all the requirements. "The main element that was missing in every case," he said; "was the database." Technology in the database arena for traditional types of database information — the kinds of applications you typically think of: inventory, billing, and so on — was mature by the end of the 1980s, but the data elements that these database products handled were also simple, when compared to documents. The technology had not grown up enough to build a text database that could feed the writing and publishing system.

So Sikorsky selected a vendor instead of a system. "We bought a system that still had to be designed and built," Richard says. "We chose the company that we believed could deliver on their promise to engineer the system we wanted." They selected their vendor in 1989 and started installing a system in 1990. Rich and members of the original team, especially Dave Rattanni, worked closely with the engineering team at the vendor over the next few years to build the system to suit their needs.

WHY SGML?

SGML was the right choice for Sikorsky for the same reasons that the DoD chose it for CALS. It provided them with a standardized way to create and manage their information, independent of how it would eventually be combined into publications for one customer or another. Using SGML to describe their technical information, Sikorsky would be able to break information down into reusable components that could be combined as needed for any one publication. SGML was the means by which they could work with information as data in a standardized electronic form rather than as words printed on paper — what Richard terms "recyclable information."

Using SGML, Sikorsky would be able to break information down into reusable components that could be combined as needed for any one publication . . . what Richard terms "recyclable information."

Richard had recognized that Sikorsky's challenge was to minimize redundancy in their published information. The documentation teams in technical support services needed a system that let them create and manage modules of information that could be used as "building blocks" for their technical publications. Richard terms this a "key reason for SGML. Proprietary formats wouldn't have let us share data in the long run," he says. "You can't insist that everybody in the whole organization use the same product to produce information. It won't happen."

SGML also gave Sikorsky a high degree of independence from its vendors. With proprietary formats, you are married to your system vendor. You have to weigh a decision to change to another product against the expense and pain involved in changing to the new manufacturer's file format. With their data in SGML, Sikorsky can adopt new software relatively easily. "Our vendor has a lot of incentive to keep Sikorsky happy," Richard observes.

"SGML was a default decision. You couldn't even put a value on it," Richard says today. "If we had not selected SGML, I don't know where we'd be today. We certainly wouldn't be able to do all the things we are doing with our documents now."

THE FINE DETAILS: HOW IT WORKS

The key accomplishment that was crucial to Rich's vision of the new system was "write once, use often." Once a writer had created some text for a helicopter, that text should automatically be in place for every subsequent set of documents that ever needed it. The only additional writing that should be needed would be the localized differences from one derivative to the next. In essence, the information about helicopters should become free of the individual documents in which it could appear.

To do this, they made two fundamental changes to the old system:

1. They reengineered the organizations that were creating the documents.
2. They changed the supporting technology.

REENGINEERING THE ORGANIZATION

As noted earlier, three different groups were responsible for writing technical documentation: Technical Publications, Training, and Logistical Support and Analysis (LSA). Over the years, these groups had evolved separately. Although their missions were distinct, they ended up rewriting large blocks of the same information. They had no way of knowing when somebody else had already written something, nor any means of capturing and reusing it.

Now that Sikorsky's system was going to be centered on a document database, where everyone could look to see if something already existed, Rich saw the opportunity to align their output more closely with their mission.

Rich reorganized the groups around the new role of "expert authors." Instead of each author being a "jack-of-all-trades" across the entire spectrum of helicopter parts and procedures, each group would now be responsible for a particular category of information, and, within the groups, authors would become subject-matter experts for different systems.

In this scheme, LSA got back to their primary mission of developing maintenance concepts and producing parts breakdowns. Training would be solely responsible for developing "theory-of-operation" documents. Technical publications was charged with writing task narratives and preparing technical illustrations.

If a writer was preparing a document that required content from another group's area of responsibility, the writer simply pointed to that document component, and it was automatically included in his text. For example, if a tech pubs writer working on a wheel-repair procedure wanted to include the parts list, the writer searched the database for that document component, which had already been developed by an LSA writer. Once located, the writer simply dropped the reference to it into his document at the place where it should appear. From that point on, the parts list would appear as part of the document, even though it was being folded in from another location in the database.

Within each of the groups, writers were assigned the responsibility for becoming system experts. In the original organization, writers had concentrated on writing for different versions of the same basic helicopter — referred to as "derivatives." One writer worked on the S70A-1, while the writer at the next desk was writing for the S70A-2 or perhaps the S70B-3. As system experts, writers found their responsibilities reassigned to focus on systems. One group of writers became specialists on the airframe, while another group focused on hydraulics and a third on avionics systems. This again helped Rich's teams write more productively and at the same time improved their consistency and accuracy. A writer who understood the hydraulics systems in depth was more likely to get it all right the first time than one who had time to understand it only superficially. And once that writer's explanation of hydraulics systems was being reused in every place where it needed to appear, the chances of two derivative helicopters having different, possibly conflicting, descriptions of the system was eliminated.

Rich found that the writers liked this arrangement better. Job satisfaction increased, because writers could focus on an area they found interesting and become proficient in it, rather than having to be satisfied with knowing a little bit about everything.

SUPPORTING THE EXPERTS WITH TECHNOLOGY

To support this new arrangement, the system the vendor was building had to deliver a text database — a central storage location where individual components of information could be stored and retrieved (see Figure 5–3).

The first step was to break down information into the lowest common denominator providing the highest efficiencies for sharing. Documents would no longer be large, undifferentiated blobs of text. They would be systematically assembled out of smaller, more coherent units of information — what the team came to call "modules." Now, Rich's team members inspected the existing documents and identified what they called the "correct granularity" for the information. These modules became the raw building blocks that, when automatically assembled by the system, became the technical documentation for a helicopter.

Within the modules, there was still the need to specify changes specific to one derivative or another. Here, they made use of an SGML construct called *marked sections*. A marked section is, as the name implies, one that has been identified for a particular purpose, such as including it in one version of a document or another. When the computer assembles the final copy for one derivative, only the marked sections identified as belonging to that helicopter are included with the common text.

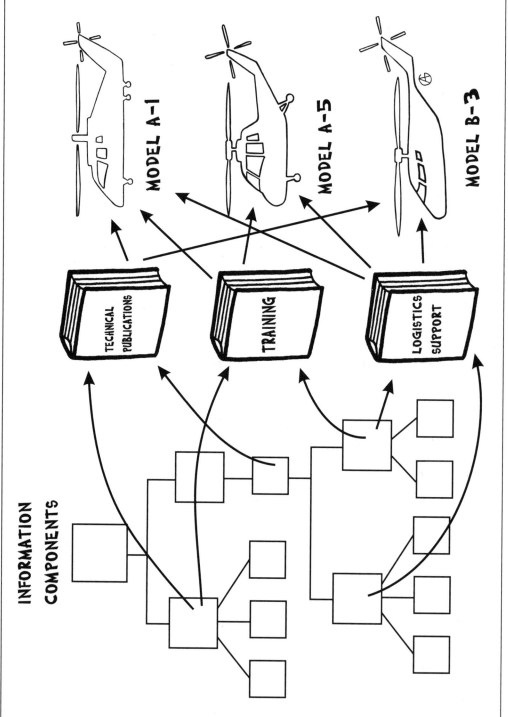

Figure 5–3. From the database, common information components can be reused for different helicopter models.

Marked sections in an SGML document might look something like this:

```
- - -
<para>The communication system controller provides control
of all modes and audio interconnections of internal and
external communications. It is located <![ %DerivativeF [
below the cockpit lower console.]]> <![ %DerivativeG [ on
the cabin avionics rack.]]>
- - -
```

In this example, if the computer was assembling a review draft for Derivative G, it would include the phrase "on the cabin avionics rack" in the copy. The phrase "below the cockpit lower console" would be ignored for Derivative G but included for Derivative F.[2]

ENHANCING THE INFORMATION'S VALUE WITH ATTRIBUTES

SGML has the ability to store additional information about the elements of a document in the start tag. This additional information is called "attributes." Attributes give you a means to store information that is about the content in addition to the content itself.

Rich's team made extensive use of this capability to enhance the value of the information they were creating. For example, they used SGML's ability to store attribute values to store the history of change requests as part of the documents themselves.

Sikorsky has to maintain a complete history of every change ever made to any of its documents for as long as that aircraft is flying. "In today's economic climate," Rich points out, "that could be 50 years!"

---

2   This is just one example of the many kinds of customized information publishing that can be accomplished using SGML. An in-depth discussion of these types of techniques can be found in *Industrial-Strength SGML: An Introduction to Enterprise Publishing* by Truly Donovan.

In the pre-SGML system, that meant holding onto a lot of paper. "There's a warehouse someplace upstate where they store all that stuff," he said.

Under the new system, the change history is stored directly in the document itself, using attribute values. Dave explained how it works. "A request for a change to a document comes to us from engineering. There's a form with a change number assigned to it and a description of the requested change. The writer enters the change in an element that we designed for that purpose, and the writer enters the change number and the engineering change-request code number as attribute values. The whole process is simple; in the SGML editor, adding a change is just another menu option.

IMPACT ON THE ORGANIZATION

How difficult was it to introduce this sophisticated, text-handling technology into Sikorsky's technical writing groups? Not particularly difficult at all.

At the time the new system was introduced, the writers were still doing most of their work by hand. Since many of the documents they had to produce were variations on books already in print, they would just write edits on existing copy. (This was one reason that the Wang system was not embraced more rapidly. Whether the writer made comments by hand or typed copy into the Wang system, the typesetter had to redo most of the text anyway, so why not just let the typesetter do the whole job from scratch?)

Richard insisted that writers be involved in the project from the beginning. Because writers from the various groups were actually leading the charge — specifying the requirements and working with the vendor to resolve problems and get the kinds of capabilities they wanted — they backed the system from the beginning. It was theirs. Or, as Rich said, "The people who have to live with this stuff day-in and day-out are the ones building the system."

"We thought changing our writers from handwriting to computers would be the biggest problem . . . it wasn't." Rich said. "It was teaching them how to type!" When he started walking around the department after the system was installed, and watching people at work, it dawned on him that many of his people had not had to learn how to type! "So we contracted with the local high school adult education department to come in and give typing lessons. Best investment we made!"

It was also one of the few formal training sessions that they had to hold. Despite the apparent high-tech nature of this new system, the writers are able to pick it up quickly because it is focused on the information, not the software program. "We originally trained about a dozen writers in SGML. It took about four hours for them to catch on, and less than a week to get them up to speed on the whole system. Since then, there has been no need for formal training." Instead, writers are trained apprentice-style. A new writer spends a week working side-by-side with an experienced writer learning the system. After that, they know just about everything they need to know. When the writer does encounter an unusual situation, the writer knows where to go to find out how to handle it.

Not everybody took to the new system, of course. But there was no demographic factor that would predict who would like it — not age, not years of experience, not seniority, not education. One writer was about to retire when they brought in SGML. "He loved it," Rich said. "He stayed here for another year because he was enjoying working with it so much."

THE PAYOFFS

Sikorsky's new system went online in 1990. Did it pay for itself? You bet! And fast: in three years, two years ahead of schedule.

Today, Richard Weich's group can point to these not inconsiderable results:

- **They have increased the department's productivity dramatically.**

  From 1987's peak of 500 writers, artists, and production people (over two thirds of them outside contractors) the department has gone to an in-house staff of 200. These 200 annually produce 60% *more* information than the 500 could ever deliver. The department no longer has a backlog, and the writers get home in time for dinner.

From a peak of 500 writers, over two thirds of them outside contractors, the department has gone to an in-house staff of 200. These 200 annually produce 60% more information than the 500 ever could.

- **They have cut the time needed to produce the finished pages to almost nothing.**

  The typesetting and cut-and-paste layout used in 1987 have been replaced by a menu option on the writer's workstation. When a manual is released for production, the system automatically assembles the modules, chooses the right marked sections, and composes finished pages. A process that once took 12 weeks now takes 12 minutes. Writers can make changes to a document right up until the day it goes to the printer. Because they ship electronic files to their printers, instead of the pasteup boards, setup time there has been reduced as well.

- **They get the most out of what each writer produces.**

  Once a chunk of information has been written, it is stored in the database and automatically reused wherever it is needed (see Figure 5–4). Sikorsky no longer has writers in different groups rewriting the same facts over and over, nor the corresponding risk of discrepancies creeping into their material.

- **They have improved the accuracy of their product.**

  The accuracy of Sikorsky's information has been significantly improved. Now, when a document is updated with new information (usually because of a request from engineering), that change will appear in every document where it belongs. Sikorsky doesn't have to make everybody stop what they are doing and track down every document where that information appeared to be sure that all their manuals are up to date.

■ **They have taken control of the cost of their operation.**

The cost of documentation for a helicopter contract has changed from a fixed cost to an incremental cost based on the volume of changes needed over and above the current database of information. For many contracts the cost is nominal, because the changes required are minor.

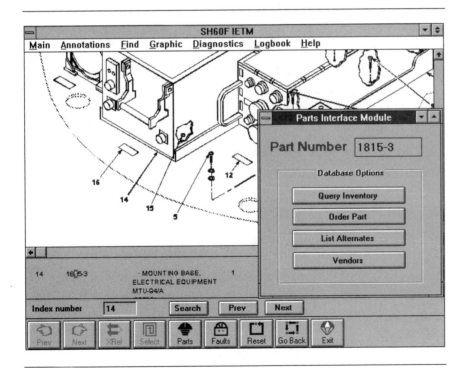

Figure 5–4. Sikorsky's Interactive Technical Manuals can even query inventory databases for parts available. *Courtesy of Sikorsky Aircraft Corporation.*

THE ELECTRONIC PRODUCTS OF THE FUTURE — TODAY

However, it is the additional products Sikorsky now produces from this database of documents that is really exciting to see — and that gives a hint at where the approach really pays off. You may not be able to put a dollar value on these benefits, but it is clear that they provide added value to both Sikorsky and its customers.

Computer-Based Training Programs

Sikorsky had been producing computer-based training programs (CBTs) for many years. By combining procedural information from the technical manuals with diagrams and animation, these programs teach technicians how to perform tasks, such as replacing a rotor assembly, outside costly classroom settings.

CBTs used to cost between $150,000 and $500,000 to develop. But by taking advantage of the structure and information stored in the SGML database, Sikorsky now has a computer program generate CBTs at one-tenth the expense. The average CBT now costs $5,000 to $25,000 to create. Because the diagrams are stored in a well-structured format, the computer is even able to generate the animation.

Interactive Electronic Technical Manuals

Interactive electronic technical manuals, or IETMs, are part of the Department of Defense's CALS initiative. An IETM is more than a simple electronic version of a paper manual. Where manuals are organized by chapter and section, IETMs must be organized by system, subsystem, and task. Figuring out how to do this cost effectively from paper-oriented word processing files has been a major stumbling block for the defense-system vendor community.

It has not been a stumbling block for Sikorsky. The information modules that combine one way to create a paper manual are simply combined another way to create an IETM. In their first test, they produced an IETM from a sample document in less than half an hour, and without making any changes to the SGML source itself.

The cost has been reduced even further by storing the information for all derivatives together on one CD. Ted Kell, the writer-turned-developer responsible for the IETMS, said; ""We used to build a separate IETM for each customer. But it is less costly and just as effective to build one IETM and just display the customer's version of the information using different filters on the data." (Remember those display filters Sybase put to such good use? Here they are again!)

Sikorsky has further enhanced their IETMs by adding sound, animation, and video to help the technician in performing maintenance tasks (see Figure 5–5).

Figure 5–5. Sikorsky replaced 20,000 pages with one CD-ROM. The first prototype was done in an afternoon.

Expert Diagnostic Systems

A major asset of any corporate or military organization is the learned knowledge and experience of its personnel. With organizations downsizing, the threat of losing such valuable experience has become a reality. In recent years, significant advances have been made in creating knowledge bases and expert systems. Using expert-system technology allows companies like Sikorsky to capture, distribute, and apply the experience of senior personnel from many disciplines on an organizationwide basis. This in turn reduces training time and improves technician performance, while lowering operational costs and mean time to repair.

However, expert systems have proved extremely expensive to develop and almost equally expensive to maintain, especially as the systems they cover grow in scope and complexity. Like the rest of the defense community, Sikorsky had been trying for several years to figure out how to deliver expert systems for troubleshooting and testing at a cost that the DoD could afford.

Once again, the answer was to recycle information, using SGML to represent the data required by the expert system software. Creating an expert-system model requires a wealth of information types:

- Test descriptions
- Preconditions and setup operations
- Time needed to perform tests
- Information about component failure rates
- Failure modes effects criticality analysis (FMECA)

Sikorsky's research proved that most of the data needed already existed in the current databases produced by publications, LSA, engineering, and so on. Representing the information in SGML and reusing it provided a very cost-effective way to develop the expert system models. It also allowed Sikorsky to use their existing database management system (DBMS).

Unlike paper manuals, using the expert system together with an IETM has distinct advantages. At each stage of the diagnosis the software computes what tests to perform next, and the IETM presents the appropriate instructions. When a faulty component is isolated, the IETM will display the repair actions that the technician should take.

Even the recording of repair actions and interfaces to inventory systems have been automated.

Because the diagnostic path is generated dynamically, it can be tuned to account for test results, user complaints, resource availability, setup operations already performed, and the like. In addition, the expert system can isolate multiple faults — paper manuals are written assuming a single fault. (A paper manual that could account for all the possible combinations of faults that the expert system can diagnose would simply be too cost prohibitive to publish.)

Tests using their prototypes showed an average 275% reduction in the time required for technicians to detect faults compared with using paper manuals.

The expert system is a real value-added product for Sikorsky customers. It turns paper "how-to" manuals into diagnosis and repair systems that interact with the technician. "We found that most companies can't afford to field systems like this because each one has to be custom developed. Ours can be tossed in with the IETMs because they just ride on top of the technical documents." Talk about competitive advantage!

Was there an easier way to achieve the same results? Rich doesn't think so. "None of this," he asserts; "would be possible without SGML."

DRAWING SOME CONCLUSIONS

Was there an easy, shrink-wrapped way to achieve the same results? Rich doesn't think so. "None of this," he asserts, "would be possible without SGML."

Rich observes, "The problem too many companies have with this subject is that management doesn't look at information as an asset. I look at it as our most important asset. How productive can people be without that library of information available to them?"

As Richard points out, the competitive edge from buildings, tools, even people, is gone. Anybody can buy the same plant, buy the same machines, hire the same people — the only discriminator many companies have any more is their intellectual capital. And the way to make the most of that sort of information is to put it into a common, neutral format that all your software programs can use.

"Most people want a magic bullet. If you don't tell them there's an easy solution, they'll just keep going around, asking the question, until someone gives them the answer they want to hear." SGML may sometimes look like a lot of work, but as the Sikorsky case shows, the payoff can be a better product for your customers and a real competitive edge, all at a much lower cost.

CHAPTER 6

Mobil Corporation

The objective wasn't to use SGML. The objective was to get control over our engineering specifications. SGML just turned out to be the best way to do it.

—Gary Sargent, Offshore Engineering Manager, Mobil Technology Company,

EXECUTIVE SUMMARY

THE GROUP

Mobil Technology Company, Exploration and Producing Technical Center.

THEIR MISSION

Coordinate all engineering and construction of oil and gas field facilities, including wells and offshore rigs.

TYPE OF APPLICATION

Engineering-specifications assembly system.

SUMMARY

For companies in the petroleum and petrochemical business, oil and gas wells and related facilities represent a major investment. Companies like Mobil spend billions of dollars each year to construct facilities all over the globe. Preparing the documents that guide the bidding and subsequent construction of these facilities has a significant impact on the total cost for these projects. A little extra-heavy-duty-gauge steel piping here, some larger-capacity pumps over there, and pretty soon you've added a few million to the bottom line.

Prior to 1993, the Mobil engineers responsible for developing engineering guides and bid documents wrote them with whatever tools were available. Although corporate standards existed, they were large and not especially easy to work with. As a consequence, engineers tended to base specifications on their own knowledge and experience. The result was a substantial amount of expensive "gold-plated" engineering that added little in the way of tangible benefits to projects.

In 1993, Mobil fielded EDEP, the Engineering Document Enhancement Program. EDEP was an automated tool that helped engineers assemble their engineering guides and bid documents. Mobil improved overall engineering quality by ensuring that company standards were met. They also lowered construction costs by reducing expensive engineering customizations.

EDEP put all industry standards — not just Mobil corporate standards — online. Delivering standards to the engineers' desktops made them far easier to reference. By putting standards at the engineers' fingertips and automating the assembly of documents, Mobil reduced the turnaround time for the engineering guides and bid documents from weeks to days, while at the same time making them more consistent from one project to the next.

GETTING A GRIP ON "GOLD-PLATING": MOBIL CORPORATION

Mobil Corporation is one of the leading oil, gas, and petrochemical companies in the world, with operations in over 100 countries. Like all oil and gas producers, Mobil invests huge sums of money each year in its production facilities such as oil wells and offshore oil rigs. Capital spending for exploration and production facilities now runs in the *billions* of dollars each year, and any single construction project can cost hundreds of millions of dollars to construct over several years.

Construction projects begin with what's called "phase I engineering," where Mobil engineers prepare a comprehensive set of engineering specifications that form a bid document. The bid document is used by construction/engineering firms like Bechtel to prepare their lump-sum bids for the work.

Bid documents are huge, typically running thousands of pages comprising hundreds of individual engineering specifications. The specifications themselves spell out in detail everything that will be required for a project, from the pipes, hoses and pumps at one end to the steel superstructures that hold it all together at the other.

The engineering specifications can have a significant impact on the eventual cost of a project. If an engineer specifies equipment or materials that exceed what the circumstances demand — for example, stainless steel pipe where carbon steel would do — then the cost of the project rises. If different parts of the spec conflict, and the problem isn't discovered until construction is underway, part of the installation may have to be torn out and rebuilt, and the cost of the project rises. If necessary information is missing from the spec and the original bid has to be revised at a later date, the cost of the project rises (see Figure 6–1).

Figure 6–1. Savings of a few percent on construction projects like this add up to millions of dollars. *Courtesy of Mobil Technology Company.*

THE BUSINESS CHALLENGE

In the past, engineers wrote engineering specifications from scratch. Typically, it took weeks, sometimes months, of work to get a bid document ready to deliver to the suppliers for bidding. Applying quality controls to the specs, although certainly something Mobil needed to do, was difficult. Each engineering center's specs looked different from the others', and each included applicable industry standards in their own way. The only way to quality check a bid document was to read it, meticulously, from page 1 to page 2001.

In the '70s and '80s, as part of its efforts to improve the quality of the documents, Mobil put corporate standards in place — hundreds of engineering guides covering every aspect of oil and gas facilities. The guides were supposed to be the basic form by which engineers drew up engineering specifications. But the guides did not prove to be all that useful.

Part of the problem was the delivery system — a shelf of ring binders that quickly became outdated if no one was assigned to insert the packages of update pages that were routinely delivered. (This has always been a big weakness when companies publish material in ring binders and then periodically send out packets of new pages to keep them up to date. Replacing all those pages in all those different binders is tedious work. Unless someone on the receiving end is made responsible for the binders, the packets of update pages pile up on the shelves next to the binders. In practice, ring-binder systems rarely stay up to date.)

Another part of the problem was the scope of the standards themselves. Much of the engineering data in the engineering guides was originally developed for offshore oil rigs in the North Sea. The North Sea is a brutal environment. (One of Mobil's largest rigs was smacked by a 100-foot wave just two weeks after it was set in place. The rig didn't even budge.) Obviously, extremely solid construction is a requirement for survival in such a locale. But those same standards are overkill for installations onshore or in more sheltered waters.

In practice, engineers often based specifications on their personal preference, rather than rely on engineering guides that they suspected were either out of date or inappropriate to their project. The result was facilities with a hefty dose of "gold-plating" — specs that exceeded the corporate standards and raised construction costs without adding any real benefits.

Exploration and production facilities are one of Mobil's core assets. Anything the company could do to maintain better quality control over the cost of construction was important to the health and competitiveness of the company. Back in Dallas, a group was beginning to think that making the engineering guides easier for the engineers to use would be a step in the right direction.

BEFORE TECHNOLOGY COMES THE PROBLEM

Mobil is a technology-oriented company and always has been. Its roots go back to 1866, when Matthew Ewing and Hiram Bond Everest's experimental method for refining kerosene produced a new petroleum lubricant instead. Since then, the company has had many firsts: Mobil products were used in the Wright brothers' early flights and on Charles Lindbergh's first solo flight across the Atlantic. Mobil developed the first synthetic automotive lubricants and oxygenated gasoline to help states meet clean-air standards.

Today, Mobil's technology initiatives are concentrated in the Mobil Technology Company (MTC). MTC's mission is to be a partner to the company's operating units and make technology bear fruit on the bottom line. Gary Sargent is part of the MTC's Exploration and Producing Technical Center (MEPTEC) in Dallas, Texas, the unit that in the late '80s was looking at the problem of improving the quality of phase I engineering. With 20-plus years of engineering assignments in the field, Gary talks about how his team looked at the problem. "People were not using the specs we had,"

Gary remembers. "There were people who didn't even know that they existed!"

Mobil has operations around the globe and every location is different — different laws, different regulations, different climates, geography, and geology. The oil, gas, and other chemicals produced and refined differ as well. Mobil believed that common standards were necessary, but partnership also meant respecting the local affiliates' knowledge about what was needed in their locations. So while there was no question that the engineering guides would continue to be produced, Gary remembers saying, "If we're going to spend the money to redevelop the engineering guides, let's make sure we make them something engineers will want to use."

The best way to do that was to let the affiliates tell MEPTEC what they felt they needed. In 1989, MEPTEC brought project engineers from around the world together in Dallas to discuss how they could make the engineering guides more useful. They asked them for their wish list.

The participants weren't shy about telling MEPTEC what they wanted. At the end of the workshop they had defined five fundamental requirements for the new engineering guides:

- Make the guides generic. Make them equally useful for on- *and* offshore installations, for the small project as well as the large. Make sure they can be customized to reflect local conditions.
- Publish the guides in an electronic form, so that they can be updated and searched more easily. Link related information together.
- Use less text and more datasheets. Don't say something in prose when it can be put in a table.
- Develop tutorials and other reference works that will help new engineers and generalists who have to get acquainted with a specific subject get quickly up to speed.
- Include industry standards online as part of the system.

MEPTEC also consulted with major industry contractors to find out what they liked and disliked about the bid documents Mobil supplied to them, with an eye toward developing final documents that the contractors would find easier to work from.

The participants left envisioning better engineering guides delivered on a CD-ROM. But what they got was something more.

SELLING THE SYSTEM

Based on the results of the workshop, the MEPTEC team put forward a project proposal. They looked at the existing engineering guides and estimated what the scope of the new guides would be. They designed some prototypes of how the new system would work and showed them to pilot groups of engineers. They came up with an estimate for a total system cost of roughly $7 million.

The project was funded not by headquarters, but by the affiliates who would use it. MEPTEC presented the proposal to the affiliates and asked each to fund a portion of the development over a three-year period. Each affiliate's share was a percentage of its capital budget. They sold it as a product — a strategic solution to a problem the affiliates wanted solved.

MEPTEC shopped around for existing solutions. Early in the project, they thought that they had found the answer when they purchased another oil company's engineering specification automation system (ESAS). The information in this system and the way it was organized appealed to Gary's team, and the system closely matched their requirements.

But months into the project, they realized that the product was too inflexible. Like Mobil, ESAS was based on the principal of corporate standards. However, it was built using a desktop publishing program and it did not allow any local modifications. "As we worked with it, we realized that the system was very rigid," Gary remembers. "All people could do was fill in datasheets and add paragraphs to the bottom of the document. Ours had to do more than that."

The information content and organization of ESAS proved to be very useful. Much of the structure of Mobil's subsequent system was derived from it. But they also needed a system that could be easily localized, could provide control over how changes to the content were made, and would provide a means of indicating what had changed in one place in the engineering guide.

So a team went out and looked for solutions. They came back with SGML.

WHY SGML?

After the experience with ESAS, the team decided that the new system should be based on open standards, not on a vendor's proprietary system. Open standards are specifications for computer languages and the like that are developed by organizations such as ANSI (the American National Standards Institute) or the ISO (the International Standards Organization). Standards produced by these organizations are their property, not the property of manufacturers of products. The standards are available to the public, and any company that chooses to support the standard in its products is free to do so.

The advantage of standards to customers is that they promote competition among manufacturers and, once a variety of products support a given standard, the customer has more freedom of choice. If a product comes out that is better than the one the customer is currently using, the customer can switch to it with little or no expense because their existing data is already in the standardized format.

This was an important issue for MEPTEC. A *big* investment was about to be made writing new engineering guides to meet their users' needs. They did not want that content locked up in a proprietary desktop publishing data format that might be made obsolete by the

A big investment was about to be made writing new Engineering Guides. They did not want that content locked up in a proprietary desktop publishing format that might be made obsolete by the manufacturer's next release.

manufacturer's next major release. SGML is an International Standards Organization (ISO) standard. Building the engineering guides on SGML protected the long-term value of that investment.

MEPTEC also wanted a solution that gave them control over the components that made up the document. In order to allow affiliates to make site-specific modifications while still protecting the content of the corporate standards, the system had to be able to control the way changes were made to engineering guides. "One of our big goals was to keep people from changing the engineering guides without any reason," Gary explains. "We wanted to be able to see what changes somebody had made just by turning to the back of the guide."

Because SGML structures a document as a collection of elements — sections, paragraphs, lists, etc. — instead of a blob of text and pictures to be printed, programs that understand SGML can control a document's elements down to whatever degree of detail the developers choose. In Mobil's case, the choice of SGML enabled them to build a system that allowed engineers to change anything in the document, but in a controlled and auditable way. A manager could review the changes made to the engineering guide just by turning to the change list at the back of the document. There, he or she would find a record of everything that had been changed, who had made the change, when, and why. "We didn't want to prevent engineers from making changes that are needed for a project," Gary says. "We just wanted to control changes that cost more money and don't add any benefit."

Mobil was also interested in finding a vendor who would work in partnership with them to build the system they envisioned. At the time they began work on the project, the SGML market was still rather small. While this meant there was some risk involved in choosing a smaller vendor, it also meant that the SGML vendors who were there were very interested in working with Mobil on the project.

By the way, this would be far less of a concern today. Faced with increasing customer demand for products that support open standards, many of the mainstream word processing and desktop publishing programs have added support for SGML into their product line. And those once niche SGML product vendors are far more "mainstream" today.

BUILDING EDEP, AN INFORMATION-ENGINEERING TOOL

In early 1991, the MEPTEC team began work on the system they were now calling EDEP, the Engineering Document Enhancement Program.

EDEP was built with an SGML authoring program that could be customized through its extensive programming capabilities. The programming language enabled them to build change controls, auditing capabilities, and other interactive features directly into the system. Mobil's vendor developed the SGML DTDs[1] and programmed their system to meet Mobil's operational requirements. "We didn't see any reason to invest in building expertise in-house for something that we expected would be a one-time thing," Gary says.

The development of the hardware and software was a small part of the overall effort. Of the $6.9 million that the system eventually cost, less than $2 million was spent on the physical system itself — and that expenditure not only covered the purchase of software, the customization of the software, and the SGML design, it also paid for the purchase of UNIX workstations for all the affiliates. (The cost would be far lower for someone building a comparable system today. In the early '90s, UNIX-based desktop publishing systems were the only ones capable of handling text and graphics simultaneously. Today, just about every desktop computer has the power to handle these tasks effectively.) Actually, $2 million doesn't look too bad, even by today's standards. "After all, we started from nothing," Gary says. "We had to build a whole publications department from the ground up."

---

1 Document type definitions (DTDs) are described in Chapter 1.

Most of the time and expense involved in building EDEP went into the activity that created the real value — writing the new engineering guides. This expense would have been the same regardless of whether the system was implemented using SGML or a proprietary product.

Creating engineering guides that the engineers would rely on and use demanded that engineers be directly involved in the development of the content. So Gary's team went out of their way to pool technical writing talent from around the globe. Every three weeks a new writing group of three to five experts would be brought together in Dallas. These teams were drawn from the ranks of facilities engineers, Mobil retirees, and even outside industry experts.

There were 180 engineering guides in all. The guides were divided into 17 categories such as heat exchangers, piping, corrosion protection, and steel structures. Each team tackled a specific guide. Their charge was to write the best guide possible based on industry standards, Mobil corporate standards, and, equally important, their own experience. In each team, a discipline leader was assigned whose job it was to coordinate schedules, handle logistics, and keep the team on track. To promote their sense of pride in authorship, each guide lists its authors.

Mobil spent two and a half years writing the guides — twelve person-years of effort by the experts — 22 writing teams per quarter for seven quarters. "At the peak," Gary recalls, "we had 30 people working in our office. It got a little crowded." In addition to the writing teams, they had technical reviewers checking the accuracy of the content, production editors reviewing the grammar, and support staff who entered the guides into the SGML system that the vendor had built.

Mobil also purchased a set of off-the-shelf tutorials from another vendor and had them edited by company specialists before converting them to SGML. Thirty-seven tutorials on specialized topics such as subsea, heavy oil, and noise control were written by Mobil teams following the general scheme of the purchased tutorials.

Existing industry standards documents were purchased from Information Handling Services (IHS), a commercial republisher of technical information and standards used by both government and industry (and another SGML user!) IHS licensed Mobil a copy of their database of industry standards. Standards, while critically important, were always a source of delays for the engineer writing a spec. Each engineering center kept copies of the standards in its office library. When an engineer needed to refer to one, a trip down the hall was in order. *If* the documents were there, and *if* the periodic packages of update pages had been consistently inserted into the proper binders, then the engineer might lose only an hour or less of productive time.

But all too often, the standards were missing or out of date. *Then* the updated materials had to be ordered. Phone calls had to be made to find the information sought. It could be anywhere from several hours to several weeks before the engineer finally had the information in hand.

EDEP's use of the IHS standards database put the standards at the engineer's fingertips. Wherever a standard was referenced in an engineering guide, that reference became an active hyperlink that would jump the engineer straight to the referenced text at a click of the mouse. This was a substantial time saver.

The first copy of the standards was straight text, a plain, typewriterlike presentation that looked pretty primitive. But IHS subsequently adopted SGML for their content, delivering it on CDs with an online SGML reader. The content then became easier to integrate with the EDEP system, and the end product looked far more sophisticated. "We sort of encouraged their interest in going in that direction," Gary says with pride.

Standards, while critically important, were always a source of delays for the engineer. EDEP put standards at the engineer's fingertips.

EDEP IN ACTION

In April of 1992 they had the first version of EDEP ready for testing. They took it out to the field in five test sites and put it to use with facilities engineers for several weeks. "We went out to the field with people and watched them use the system," Gary recalls. "You have to do that if you want it to be a system people will use, because until you do that, the system is just your best guess as to how it ought to work. When we watched engineers use the system and talked to them about what worked and what didn't, we quickly found out there were about five things that we had guessed wrong on."

After refining the interface and the operation based on what they had learned, MEPTEC rolled out EDEP, Version 1.0, in April of 1993. Since then they have issued biennial releases upgrading the system.

The result is the EDEP User's System — 15,000 printed pages and eight feet of shelf space that now ships on one CD-ROM and, for most sites, can be routinely updated over the network. The EDEP User's System has four components:

- The E&P engineering guides written by the teams of experts.
- The E&P tutorials.
- Online standards documents, including MQSM, the Mobil Quality Standards Manual that provides quality control information for tubular goods, i.e., pipes. Pipes, as you can imagine, are a pretty hefty chunk of the money an oil company spends. "The MQSM was added because some other folks at Mobil saw what we were doing and saw how they could apply it to what they wanted to do," Gary says.
- The E&P site specific engineering guides. These are versions of the main E&P guides that local engineers have customized to reflect local conditions and requirements.

EDEP is a completely online tool. The original release was supplied to the affiliates both on paper and on CD-ROM. As new engineering guides are added to the product, printed copies are still sent to the affiliates.

MORE THAN JUST A REFERENCE BOOK

But EDEP is more than just an electronic version of the guides and tutorials. It is more than just an online reference document for engineers to read. EDEP is the tool that they use to build bid documents.

The E&P engineering guides and the site-specific guides serve as the basic templates for creating bid documents. Creating site-specific guides is managed by EDEP as well (see Figure 6–2).

To create a site-specific version of the lube and seal oil system, for example, an engineer selects that guide from a list and then selects "make site specific" from the EDEP system's menu. EDEP retrieves a copy of the guide from its online library and opens it.

The original engineering guide remains in the library unchanged. EDEP automatically changes the designation on this new copy from "EPG" (E&P engineering guide) to "EPS" (E&P engineering guide — site specific). It also adds a proviso to the beginning of the document explaining that this is a localized document, adapted from a Mobil engineering guide, that contains "a detailed and precise statement of requirements, materials, dimensions, and workmanship" that can be used as the foundation for a set of engineering specifications.

This copy of the guide can now be modified to reflect local conditions and requirements. However, the engineer still cannot make just any edits to the document the way he or she could in a word processor. EDEP allows changes to be made — but in a controlled and auditable way.

To change the content of a section, the engineer chooses "delete section" from the EDEP menu. In reality, the section is *not* deleted; instead, it is flagged as having been changed and is hidden from view on the screen and in printouts. The original content always remains with the document as a point of comparison.

When the first change is made to the guide, an addendum titled "Site-Specific Information" is added to the back of the document. From then on, copies of each "deleted" section are placed there. A cross-reference referring the reader to this addendum is also placed where a section originally appeared in the document. The copy of a

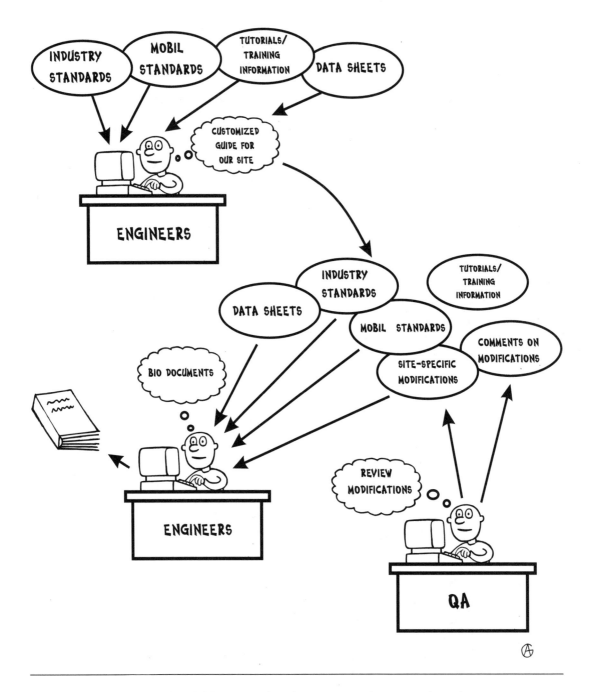

Figure 6–2. EDEP Engineering Guides are not just documents — they are tools engineers use to create bid documents.

section in the site-specific addendum *can* be freely edited by the engineer, and this is where the engineer makes localized changes.

The EDEP also adds a table titled "Revision Log" at the end of the guide. Information about every change made to the document is recorded there: who made the change, when, and why. To review the changes to the guide, a manager no longer must read the entire document. Instead, he or she can flip to the back page, refer to the revision log, and see a concise list of all the alterations to the corporate standards.

This feature alone has helped cut the volume of "personal-preference" engineering changes tremendously. "You know, you take a 40-page document and the only way you can find out what somebody changed is to read all the way through it, you're going to be tempted to just sign off on the thing and get on with your work," Gary observes. "But if you can just look in the back, find a list of all the changes, and check them right there on the spot, now you are definitely going to do it."

The change-control feature has another benefit as well. The revision logs and site-specific addendums from the affiliates give MEPTEC valuable feedback about the corporate standards. If a guide has errors or omissions or if a corporate standard needs to be reviewed, MEPTEC can see that in the site-specific changes. Those changes can be made to the main E&P engineering guides and quickly be made available to the rest of the affiliates. EDEP also includes a User's System Response Form, an integrated response system through which engineers can inform the MEPTEC developers of needed changes to the guides. The response form is emailed directly from the engineer's desktop back to MEPTEC's EDEP development team.

DEVELOPING A BID DOCUMENT

The process of creating a bid document is similar to creating site-specific engineering guides. The guides themselves form the standard specifications that go out with the bids. For each category of information, either the standard engineering guide or the site-specific guide is part of the final bid document.

An engineer working on a part of the bid document can also add addenda to the guides to address additional issues such as special warranties. One type of document frequently added is a technical datasheet.

Datasheets are forms that provide precise information for specific devices, such as pumps or generators. They are detailed documents that specify operating conditions, site data, instrumentation requirements, etc. for each type of device needed on the project. Datasheets form the bulk of a bid document.

In the past, filling in the datasheets was a time-consuming process. Redundant information had to be filled in over and over again. Specific values and acceptable ranges had to be checked. As part of the EDEP system, MEPTEC turned datasheets into "intelligent forms."

Now an engineer has to supply an item of information only once — it will automatically be used whenever it is called for. For example, once an item's name and number have been entered, the name and number will automatically be filled in anywhere on the forms that it is called for.

As the engineer creates the datasheet, he only needs to fill in the blanks. If a specific item of information is required and the engineer leaves it blank, a message pops up to inform the engineer that it is missing. As the datasheets are created, this feature makes it possible to audit the bid document and make certain it is complete.

Fields having acceptable values or ranges of values have that information programmed into the form. If an engineer wants a reminder of what values are acceptable for a box on the form, the answer can be popped up. And if the engineer enters a value that falls outside the accepted norms, a pop-up box reminds the engineer of the standards. The engineer can still override the recommendation if he chooses to, but engineers no longer have to be concerned that they are using the wrong information unknowingly.

In addition to the hyperlinked standards, the engineering guides and datasheets also contain comments that explain the reasoning behind a specification and additional considerations to take into account when modifying the specification. These comments are extremely useful to the engineers, but they are not appropriate content to forward to vendors. The EDEP system allows the comments to be hidden at any time, such as when printing the bid document for a vendor.

HOW SGML MAKES EDEP POSSIBLE

When asked whether the EDEP system could have been done without using SGML, Gary answers, "I don't know what else would have given us that kind of control over the contents of the documents."

Look at just some of what the EDEP system does:

1. It allows engineers to localize documents, but controls the way changes are made to them.
2. It provides an audit trail for the document, recording every change that is made.
3. It enters repeated information automatically.
4. It tests documents to make sure they are complete, and it tests data that has been entered against acceptable values.

To build capabilities like these into a document engineering system like EDEP, the software must be able to identify the individual elements of a document. It must know what elements are required and what elements are optional. It must be able to store associated information, such as allowable pressure ranges or viscosity values, with the boxes in a form where those values are supplied. In short, the software must know something about the structure of the document.

SGML is the only standard that allows software developers like EDEP's developers to define the structure of a document and then use that structure to their advantage. For example, when an engineer using EDEP wants to change the text in a section, the system must be able to distinguish the section chosen from the text that comes before it and the text that comes after it. Word processing and desktop publishing systems don't store that kind of information about a document. They only store a continuous stream of instructions for printing the document.

SGML, by defining the document's elements explicitly, provided the necessary backbone on which EDEP could be built. Many products could be used to deliver EDEP as an electronic book on CD-ROM, with varying degrees of ease and success. But SGML was the key capability that made it possible to build EDEP as an engineering tool.

THE PAYOFF

EDEP has definitely saved Mobil money. However, Gary sees no pressing reason to precisely quantify the savings. "EDEP's not here to help us make money," he says. "It's here to help us do a better-quality job. Even if it has saved just 1% off what projects otherwise would have cost us, it paid for itself in the first year of operation. One percent of hundreds of millions of dollars is a lot of money."

Mobil got one big payoff from SGML that will never show up on the balance sheets — their $5 million investment in Engineering Guides and Tutorials is protected from future changes in computer hardware and software.

Mobil got one big payoff from basing EDEP on SGML that will never show up on the balance sheets, but which nevertheless will benefit the company for years to come — their $5 million investment in engineering guides and tutorials is protected from changes in computer hardware and software.

With typical word processing programs, your documents can be used reliably only with the program that created it. If you want to change to a new program, the cost of converting to the new program's format will likely be extremely high. And many companies have made substantial investments in building document-management systems using word processing programs, only to have the systems "broken" by the changes in the next major upgrade to the product.

"I suppose we could have tried to build EDEP with a word processing program," Gary says. "But if the program was changed or the company went out of business, where would we be?"

By building the system on SGML, Mobil has ensured that they can migrate EDEP to new versions of software in the future at a reasonable cost. They can also expand the reach or the capabilities of EDEP by bringing in other software that can also handle SGML. One way they have already done that is by delivering the EDEP system on a CD-ROM to small satellite offices that use personal computers instead of UNIX workstations. "Just having the CD on a PC for reference helps engineers out in the smaller satellite offices," Gary states.

EDEP and SGML have resulted in other substantial benefits to Mobil as well:

- **They have significantly reduced the amount of "gold-plated engineering" in their bid documents and, as a result, achieved capital savings on their projects.**

  By making Mobil's corporate standards an interactive part of the tool the engineers use to write engineering specifications, MTC has made it painless for engineers to stick to the standards. Engineers can change the standards where they feel they need to do so, but now those changes can be tracked and managed.

- **They have saved money by shortening the time required to turn around engineering specifications and bid documents.**

  First, they don't write them from scratch. Second, they don't lose time looking for standards. Third, technical datasheets have been turned into intelligent forms that help the engineer fill them out. The result is that bid documents that used to take weeks to complete are now usually finished in a matter of days.

- **And the quality of the final product is better.**

  When engineers wrote their specs from scratch, each engineering specification was different. The differences varied from the minor to the major. But the end result was that every engineering specification was a custom document. It look longer to

By making Mobil's standards an interactive part of the tool the engineers use to write engineering specifications, MTC has made it painless for engineers to stick to them.

review internally and longer for the suppliers to review for the bid. "What we hear from our contractors is that having the specifications in a consistent format and organization saves you money on the project. They tell us that it can cut as much as 10% off the cost of the job," Gary says.

- **They have significantly cut the number of "redos."**

  Redos happen when something specified in one part of the spec conflicts with something specified in another part of the spec and the discrepancy isn't discovered until construction is underway. "Redos are *real* expensive," Gary says, "because you build it once, then you end up having to tear it down and build it again the right way."

  With the EDEP system, Mobil captures the learning from errors. Redos caused by inaccuracies in the engineering guides don't happen twice. "When we find out about a mistake," Gary says, "we figure out what caused it and fix it in the EDEP data. The next update that goes out to the field distributes the fix with it, and that mistake doesn't happen twice."

- **They have reduced the cost of direct engineering supervision by providing the online tutorials, and they have also captured expertise and experience that was being lost when engineers retired.**

  Gary points out that EDEP "is a good technology-transfer tool." Every time an experienced engineer retires or leaves the company, Mobil loses years of experience and expertise. When they wrote the E&P tutorials, Mobil brought in many of those senior engineers as well as retirees to be their technical experts. The tutorials, linked directly into the engineering guides, now provide the benefits of those engineers' years of learning to the new engineers just starting out.

There is another payoff from adopting SGML that has only recently made itself evident. In response to changes in both the organization and technology, MTC is updating EDEP's delivery system. One appealing approach is the use of intranets and World Wide Web technology, a solution can enable even better interaction between users and technical specialists. Gary observes that, "It seems about the time we get a system in place and running well, it's time to start looking at new methods. Change is something we must deal with constantly."

Converting the volume of information in the EDEP system's engineering guides, tutorials and industry standards into HTML, the underlying markup language of the World Wide Web, would have been an enormously expensive proposition had the content been authored using conventional format-oriented word processors. And keeping HTML versions of the content up-to-date as the Web keeps evolving would be an ongoing expense. By having that content in SGML, MTC can opt instead to plug the data directly into the Web, using converters to create HTML on-the-fly, whenever a user wants to read a document. Implementing — and maintaining — a new delivery system will be substantially easier.

MEPTEC did a lot of things right when they built the EDEP system. They brought the engineers who would eventually use the system in right from the start; they drew on the experience and knowledge of users to write the new engineering guides; they field tested EDEP with a large group of engineers to test their assumptions before they rolled it out to the field.

Relying on SGML was one of those "right" decisions. SGML was a small part of the project in terms of the dollars spent, but it was a key decision, because it was the backbone that made EDEP's benefits possible.

CHAPTER 7

The Semiconductor Industry

*We have the advantage of being in an industry that's young,
an industry that was started by very smart people. The people who
founded it and drive it today are used to thinking about technology problems.*

—Bob Yencha, Senior Systems Analyst, National Semiconductor.

*I once said I'd probably be fired for suggesting a project like this.
My manager said to me, 'You ought to be fired if you **don't**.'*

—Jeff Barton, Information Systems and Applications
Support Manager, Texas Instruments.

EXECUTIVE SUMMARY

THE MEMBERS

Hitachi America, Ltd., Intel Corporation, National Semiconductor, Philips Semiconductors, Texas Instruments Semiconductor Group.

THEIR MISSION

Develop an industry information standard to support the development of electronic semiconductor data books, comprehensive collections of information about "chips."

TYPE OF APPLICATION

Industry standard for information interchange.

SUMMARY

The semiconductor industry is one of the most powerful economic engines of the 20th century, generating $150 billion in annual sales and employing tens of thousands of people worldwide. Yet, despite all its high-tech accomplishments, the industry continues to create and publish documentation using traditional word processing and desktop publishing tools.

This would be fine if the volume of information the manufacturers need to provide to users was relatively static, relatively finite, and relatively manageable. It is anything but. The volume of information that customers need in order to find, choose, test and use semiconductor chips is exploding, driven by geometric increases in the complexity of

chips themselves, and the information never stands still for very long. Traditional publishing methods that simply fix words on paper (or its electronic equivalent) can no longer cope with the churning avalanche of information these companies are producing.

Five semiconductor companies have teamed up to invent, not a new chip, but a revolution in chip-documentation technology. They have developed a draft standard for semiconductor information that represents a new database-style approach to capturing and transmitting this content. In the process, they have improved their internal processes significantly and enhanced their ability as organizations to capture and distribute data to their customers.

Aviation and aerospace, automotive, petrochemical, financial, pharmaceutical — many industries today are wrestling with the impacts of the information explosion. (And ironically, by making it ever easier and cheaper to create paper, computers have made the problem worse instead of better!) How *these industries* respond to the new economics of information will have a profound impact on how successful they are going into the 21st century. The member companies of the Pinnacles Initiative may have recognized the problem first, but they are showing all of us what it will take to address these problems in our own businesses.

TACKLING THE INFORMATION EXPLOSION AT HITACHI, INTEL, NATIONAL SEMICONDUCTOR, PHILIPS SEMICONDUCTORS, AND TEXAS INSTRUMENTS

An advertisement from Intel Corporation, the company whose microprocessors drive a large percentage of the world's personal computers, features a 1950s technology magazine's then amazing prediction that "One day computers will weigh less than a ton." The humorous point of the ad, of course, is just how amazingly right the prediction has turned out to be (and yet how amazingly little of the weight reduction it actually predicted).

Consider the ENIAC (Electronic Numerical Integrator and Computer), generally acknowledged to be the first successful modern digital computer. Invented at the University of Pennsylvania's Moore School of Electrical Engineering in 1946, it weighed 30 tons. It was also 100 feet long, 8 feet tall, used 18,000 vacuum tubes and 170,000 resistors, and drew 180 kilowatts whenever it was turned on.

As chips themselves get smaller and more powerful, the information required to make use of them explodes.

As part of the 50th anniversary celebration for ENIAC, a group of graduate and undergraduate students led by Dr. J. Van der Spiegel and Dr. F. Ketterer faithfully recreated ENIAC on a single semiconductor chip. Dr. Van der Spiegel says that the "ENIAC-on-a-Chip" project "dramatically illustrates the performance improvements brought about by semiconductor technology."[1] And how! The ENIAC chip completely reproduces both the functions and the design of its ancestor on a sliver of silicon about six-tenths of an inch square. It uses a mere one-half watt of power — not even enough to make a light-bulb filament glow. Although it models the original ENIAC's design exactly, it is 200 times faster. And it doesn't weigh much more than a contact lens! (See Figure 7–1).

---

1 "ENIAC-on-a-Chip" by Jan Van der Spiegel, *PENNPRINTOUT*, The University of Pennsylvania's computing magazine, March 1996.

Figure 7–1. The original ENIAC computer took up a room of its own. The microchip measures less than an inch. Photo of ENIAC courtesy of *Archives of the University of Pennsylvania.* Photo of ENIAC chip courtesy of *University of Pennsylvania Moore School of Electrical Engineering.*

"ENIAC-on-a-Chip" is just one dramatic example of why semiconductors are changing so many aspects of our lives. The personal computers on our desktops are orders of magnitude more powerful than the mainframe computers businesses relied on in the 1960s and 70s. But only 10% of the semiconductors manufactured annually end up in computers. The rest are in our phones and our kitchen appliances. They are in our kids' sneakers and the brakes on our cars. They are even in our pets. (I kid you not! Schering-Plough, the American pharmaceutical company, is marketing HomeAgain™, a rice-grain-sized semiconductor that, when implanted under an animal's skin between the shoulder blades, permanently stores identifying information with the pet. Sort of like "Bar codes for Bonzo.") (See Figure 7–2).

The irony of the semiconductor business is that, as the chips themselves get smaller and more powerful, the information required to make use of them explodes. The data books which communicate the technical information about chips are usually the size of city telephone directories, and even then they are incomplete.

Just as semiconductors are the leading edge of industrial technology, the industry's problems in handling the information side of its business are a leading indicator of what other industries face in the coming years, as customers demand faster, broader access to more and more product and services information. Analyzing this industry's information challenges and its response to them is like looking through a crystal ball into our own futures.

Figure 7–2. A semiconduct chip that is injected under the skin can permanently identify your pet.

THE BUSINESS CHALLENGE

Semiconductors are one of the 20th century's acknowledged miracle devices. The industry got its start in 1947 when scientists at Bell Labs invented the transistor — a small device made from silicon that quickly replaced the vacuum tube as the guts of electronic equipment. It was transistors that made the world of high technology possible. They were smaller and more rugged than vacuum tubes while requiring a lot less power. Without transistors, most of the technological developments of the following decades simply could not have happened. No space program, no computer revolution, no cable television, audio CDs, or wireless cellular phones. The transistor is the grandparent of all these inventions.

The industry made a quantum leap forward in the 1960s when a team of scientists developed a photolithograhic process for etching transistors and circuits onto thin sheets of silicon. It was similar to enlarging a photograph, only in reverse. The integrated circuit, or IC, gave the industry an enormous productivity boost. Now, instead of physically soldering transistors onto plastic circuit boards, a company could design an integrated circuit and then reproduce it the way a photo lab prints pictures. ICs made mass production of electronic products possible.

In 1968 the industry made its next quantum leap when a Japanese firm named Busicom asked a new company called Intel to design a set of chips for a calculator. Intel responded with a design that collected all the functions of a calculator on a single chip. The result, introduced in 1971, was the Intel 4004 — the first microprocessor. "Micro" because of its size — about the same as a child's fingernail. "Processor" because it brought together in one chip not just transistors and their connections, but also the memory, the clocks, the programming logic — everything needed to make it a general-purpose electronic product. The 4004 was the first example of a computer on a single chip.

The growing complexity of semiconductors has made the information side of the business increasingly difficult, because customers need access to an enormous volume of information about a chip in order to find it, choose it, test it, and use it. Who are these customers? Well, they are the companies and the engineers who use chips to build products you and I will buy — from greeting cards, cellular telephones, and microwave ovens to medical diagnostic equipment, air traffic control systems, and Bonzo's bar-code chip. With the right information, they can turn semiconductors into dazzling, cutting-edge products. Without the information, those same chips are just tiny blobs of plastic, silicon, and wire.

How much information are we talking about here? Plenty! The complexity of semiconductors *doubles* every year and a half, a rate of change known as Moore's Law after Dr. Gordon Moore, one of the co-founders of Intel. In 1965, when he published that observation, the microprocessor had not yet been invented. Semiconductors were still simple enough that a savvy engineer could "clip the chip" — solder a bit of wire between two of its pins to tweak its operating characteristics. The most advanced ICs were squeezing a few thousand transistors at most onto a piece of silicon 0.5 cm (3/16 inch) square. Yet Dr. Moore predicted it would take less than 20 years to bump that number up over one million — something many in the industry didn't even believe possible. But he was right. The first microprocessor, Intel's 4004, had 2,300 transistors. Today's Intel Pentium® Pro processor chip has 5.5 million! And nobody expects Moore's Law to stop applying to the business anytime soon.

As the complexity of semiconductors goes, so goes the volume of information a customer needs in order to use them. Data books — the primary reference source for a chip — can easily run into the thousands of pages of datasheets, application notes, diagrams, and tables describing hundreds of operations, signals, inputs, and outputs that the chip can handle. *Yet even those thousands of pages are incomplete, because it is literally impossible, using traditional tools and methods, to get all the information into print.* Data books are at best only a snapshot of the information a customer might need to know. And errors and inconsistencies in the content are a significant problem. Data books are assumed to be out of date before they get off the printing press.

With the right information, engineers can turn semiconductors into dazzling products. Without the information, those same chips are just tiny blobs of plastic, silicon, and wire.

THE TROUBLE'S IN THE TOOLS

The crux of the problem is that while the volume of information about chips has exploded, driven by advances in the tools engineers use to develop them, the tools used to publish that information have changed very little. In the '70s, engineers were still manually creating circuits by etching them onto templates with X-Acto blades. Today, engineers let their fingers do the walking, using modeling tools and computer-aided-design (CAD) software to produce chips many orders of magnitude more complex. But they still use word processors to write information down.

Information is being created and changed so rapidly that the old "words on paper" method of recording information has been overwhelmed.

Not that word processors and desktop publishing packages have not gotten better, mind you. They have; but they are still just tools for putting words down, one after another, on paper. Which would be fine:

- If the time-to-market window weren't getting shorter and shorter all the time (but it is).
- If complex, interconnected data about connections, signals, performance, and so on weren't changing constantly during the product development cycle (but it is).
- If large portions of the information weren't being generated automatically by computer programs in formats useful to automated design tools but useless to word processors (but they are).
- If different groups and departments within the organization weren't using different computer systems and software that are largely incompatible with one another (but they are).

The information is being created and changed so rapidly that the old "words-on-paper" method of recording information has been overwhelmed. The traditional writing methods just can't keep up any longer.

For the manufacturers, paper-oriented methods of producing books are too slow and cumbersome. Competitive pressures and advances in technology are making their time-to-market window shorter and shorter.

Chips that used to be upgraded every six months now turn around every six weeks. Consider the $1.5-*billion* fabrication plants used to manufacture Intel's Pentium® chips, the current state of the art for Windows personal computers. It has been reported that they will be completely amortized in just two years. The industry cannot afford traditional methods for developing chip documentation; it needs a revolution in the tools that capture, manage, and deliver information.

For the customers, data books are hard to work with. Every manufacturer's books come in a different format and include (*and* skip over) different information. Engineers have no way to search through chip information with any precision, so all too often they live with the chip they manage to locate and fudge their product design to make it fit. (This is a reality that SGML is already changing. See the discussion of Krakatoa™ at the end of this chapter.)

The harder it is to search for the right chip, and the harder it is to wade through a data book to find the chip's operating characteristics, the longer it takes the users to get their products to the market. The customers want information delivered in an electronic form, faster and more accurately, and they want to be able not just to read it, but to pull it into their computer-aided-design systems as well.

These are problems that the industry wants to solve. The reason is that semiconductor manufacturers who deliver complete and accurate information to their customers in a form that is easy to search and use will have a real competitive advantage in the decades ahead.

THE BEGINNINGS OF A SOLUTION

People in the industry have been working on these problems for years. Two of those people are Bob Yencha, senior systems analyst with National Semiconductor, and Pat O'Sullivan, strategic publishing process manager at Intel. Bob and Pat were actively involved in a volunteer industry group (the "Electronic Data Book Working

Group") that was looking for ways to publish data books in an electronic form. But in the late '80s and early '90s the group's success had been limited, hampered by the ad hoc way that data books are created in the first place. "We kept showing up at all the same conferences," Pat recalls. "The more we kicked things around, and talked about the problems we faced, the more we realized that we all shared common problems."

In 1990, Bob and Pat were attending a conference in Boston. At the time, they thought what the industry needed was a standard data-book format, but they knew that it was not a practical solution. Getting every company in the industry to agree to publish the same information the same way would be next to impossible. While at the conference, they attended an SGML session taught by the late Yuri Rubinsky, one of SGML's most eloquent advocates, and they came out with a new idea. "We were thinking that we needed a set of formats that everyone would agree to use," Bob says. "But then some of us saw a presentation on SGML and we went from thinking 'tag library' to thinking 'information architecture.'"

Over the coming months, they discussed the idea with counterparts at other companies and found they had kindred spirits in the industry. At a conference in Florida, they hooked up with Alfred Elkerbout, manager of product information development at Philips Semiconductors. Philips was already using its first generation of SGML systems, and Pat recalls how they "tossed around ideas for working together. When we suggested datasheets as a category of documents to analyze, his ears picked right up." Next, they hooked up with Jeff Barton, information systems and applications support manager at Texas Instruments. "The way we saw it at TI, people were using our products as plug and play components to build impressive systems. We needed to have plug and play information too," Jeff says. "It was as if, having all individually come to the decision to use SGML, we then found each other."

WHY SGML?

Each company had come to SGML for its own reasons. But each was responding to the same essential pressures: customer demand for electronic access, a deluge of rapidly changing information, heterogeneous corporate computing environments, and what Tom Jeffrey of Hitachi called "the level playing field. We want our customers to see our data in the same format or the same system where they see the data from all the other manufacturers."

They had concluded that the solution they needed would provide certain key characteristics:

1. It must be system and vendor independent. If the solution had to run on one computer, or was built by one particular computer vendor, then it could not solve their problems because everyone — semiconductor vendors, suppliers, and customers — had and would continue to have a wide array of different environments.

2. It must be able to integrate or reference other standards. The semiconductor industry is driven by standards, and a great deal of research goes on every day into developing more ways of modeling the behavior of chips before they are actually manufactured and of automating design tools to mimic how those chips will behave in other products. Companies were looking for ways to merge the information from data books directly into such modeling and design tools.

3. It must be supported by commercially available tools and services so that solutions could be rapidly implemented.

4. It must protect the data against changes in document development and delivery systems. The information about a chip represented a substantial investment on the part of the manufacturer. They did not want solutions that tied that data so closely to tools that the information could be made obsolete by a change in the technology.

5. It must support current paper and electronic publishing processes while providing an avenue to take advantage of new processes when they arise.

Alfred Elkerbout pointed out another advantage that Philips saw in adopting SGML. "We were looking for increased accuracy and improved consistency for our data right from the very first moment in the product's design life cycle," he says. "Then we could carry that information, enriching it throughout the corporation, right up until it is actually delivered to the customer."

Given the requirement for open information that could be shared, enriched and exchanged across a diverse collection of hardware and software, there was only one possible choice: SGML

Given these requirements for open information that could be shared, enriched, and exchanged across as diverse a collection of hardware and software as exists in any industry, there was only one possible choice: SGML.

THE PINNACLES INITIATIVE: INVENTING A REVOLUTION

In 1992 Bob, Pat, Alfred, and Jeff made an unusual proposal to the CAD Frameworks Initiative (CFI), an industry standards-making organization and sponsor of the Electronic Data Book Working Group. Their four companies would fund the development of an industry information standard for semiconductor data books, outside the framework of the CFI's normal operation. "The Working Group had the usual problems of a volunteer organization," Pat recalls. "People would come to one meeting and then not to the next, so it was very difficult to move things forward." Bob adds, "We were convinced that this had to be a funded effort if it was going to get anything accomplished."

The CFI's board agreed. After the meeting, the group drove up to Pinnacles National Monument, a park famous for its spiky peaks and jagged rock formations. Unwinding amidst the natural splendor, they outlined their game plan and planned their next steps. Alfred was taking snapshots of the scenery when somebody asked, "What are we going to call this project?" He said, "How about 'Pinnacles?'" and the undertaking had a name.

In April 1993 Intel, National Semiconductor, Philips Semiconductors, and Texas Instruments signed the agreement that officially created the "Pinnacles Group," an organization whose mission was to produce the "Pinnacles Component Information Standard" or PCIS. (Hitachi joined in 1994, while the initial analysis phase was still underway.) The group turned to ATLIS Consulting, an SGML consulting company that had helped them earlier in the project by developing an SGML workshop for interested members of the CFI.

Tommie Usdin, who was then at ATLIS, remembers that "the Peaks" (as the group members came to be called) did two very important things right at the beginning. They wrote up a detailed set of goals *and* nongoals — they were just as clear about what Pinnacles would *not* be as they were about what it would. And they wrote a detailed first-year project plan, right down to the number of engineers that would be needed for analysis workshops."

"Pinnacles had a philosophy from the start," Pat explains. "We weren't going to tell anybody what they had to put in a data book or how they had to make it look. All we said was, '*If* you put this piece of information in a data book, then *this* is what you call it *when* you exchange it with someone else.'" In effect, what Pinnacles set out to define was a level playing field for everybody's information that everyone could count on.

ANALYZING THE PROCESS OF PRODUCING INFORMATION

The Pinnacles game plan called for a series of week-long workshops, one at each of the member companies and one final reconciliation workshop at the end. The workshops would analyze typical datasheets, application notes, and data books, define the information components they contained, and describe how they related to one another. After they had consensus on the information content of the documents, ATLIS would formalize the standard in SGML.

Most of the participants at the workshops were to be engineers, product managers, technical writers, marketing communications people — content experts from every group in the company that created information or used it. It was these people's time that represented the largest investment of the member companies. Each company agreed to commit their best engineers to the workshops — a total of roughly 7 ½ person-years spread over 12 months and worth approximately $2.1 million. There were also observers from the other member companies and from the host company.

When engineers heard they would spend a week describing data sheets, they would all but laugh out loud. By the third day, the atmosphere had changed!

LESSONS FROM THE MASTERS

Tommie Usdin calls the method that they use in the workshops "Mud, Bricks, and Mud. The first workshop stirs up a whole lot of mud and out of that you make a few bricks," she says. "The second takes the mud left from the first, makes more bricks, stirs up more mud, and so it goes."

There were five workshops in all, and the progress was always the same. When the engineers heard that they would be spending a week describing what goes into a data sheet, they would all but laugh out loud. Jeff Barton remembers that "The prevailing notion was 'it's just a data sheet . . . it's easy.'" Participants were alternately irritated at losing a week from their *real* work and skeptical that they would learn anything from the exercise.

Then they began talking about what went into datasheets and they started to stir up some mud. By the third day of the workshop, the atmosphere had changed. The engineers had decided that something worthwhile was going on, and they realized that they weren't going to be able to finish the analysis. They started asking, "Why aren't we working 12 hours instead of just 10?" They volunteered to keep going over the weekend. "Their biggest frustration," Tommie recalls, "was that they wouldn't finish. Every workshop group wanted to be the one who got the job done."

Why the change? Well, one reason was that datasheets turned out to be far more complicated than any of them had imagined. For example, there was the "any-idiot" principle. In the push to get a semiconductor documented so that the chip can get to the market, engineers often leave out information they feel is obvious. A datasheet might include the equation $V_{CC} = MIL$, but nowhere in the datasheet is MIL defined or its value given. In the workshops, when asked about such omissions, engineers typically said, "Well, any idiot would know that." Tommie recounts how she handled these situations. "I would ask which experts in the room would be expected to know the answer. Then I would hand them each a folded sheet of paper and ask them to write down the value that 'any idiot would know.' If you had 12 subject-matter experts in the room, you generally got 12 different answers!"

"It turned out," she adds, "that a large part of the calls the companies get to customer support are for those pieces of information that "any idiot would know." Engineers who could be at work on product designs instead spend valuable time doing phone support.

However, there was another key reason for the change. What was novel about the workshop setting was that, for the first time, engineers were looking at the information that was published about their chips as both information creators *and* as information consumers. As creators, they had always thought they had it down cold. But in the workshops they saw, for the first time, the relationship between what they produced on the one hand, and what they got from each other's companies on the other. Engineers began to say to themselves "Sure, I'll produce my data this way because when I get *your* data it will be this way too."

The participants were seeing datasheets in a new way — not as pieces of paper but as packages of information. "We kept the discussions at a high level — the name of this information, and the nature of it,"

Tommie says. "We didn't let it turn into arguments about how the page should look." And the engineers began to recognize the possibility to receive and use the data in a whole new way. They were suddenly in their customers' shoes, and what excited them was the idea that they could get their hands on data in a form that they could not only read but could plug straight into the design process.

THE AUTHORING PROCESS
TURNS OUT TO BE A MESS

Meanwhile, the Peaks were getting a good look at the process of creating datasheets. It wasn't a pretty sight. "At first we were embarrassed at the holes we kept finding," Bob remembers. "But then we realized that none of us was doing it right! We were looking not only at what information we produced, but also at our processes for producing it, and we weren't exactly happy with what we saw."

They discovered that there were *enormous* differences in how different groups create information, even within the same company. "Each group used whatever system they felt was optimum for their work," Bob explains. "The concept people might use PCs, while design engineers used high-end UNIX workstations. Then the info went back out to the manufacturing and test folks, who happen to use both, and to the marketing people, who use Macs. A data book was supposed to survive the trip through all of those different systems. In fact, what we learned was that from the time we conceived a datasheet to the time we delivered it to the customer, it was being retyped four times."

It was the same for all of them. Pat recalls how at Intel, as a result of what they discovered at the workshops, they assigned a summer intern to study what it took to get a typical data book from creation to customer. The intern followed the documentation for two major product lines and spot-checked a few others. "He found that almost half the cost of a data book was in the creation," Pat says. "And he discovered that the creation stage included a lot of activities that were huge time sinks. For example, there was the time an engineer would spend searching for the right information that he could reuse if only he could figure out where it was. Or there was the time he would spend retyping information because although he found it, it was in the wrong format, or it only existed on a piece of paper in somebody's desk drawer. Or worst of all, he would find four different versions of data, and then have to spend time figuring which of the four was current — if any!"

"That's why everybody still uses paper today," Bob concludes. "It is the only thing everybody knows how to handle." But that is also why SGML is such a cornerstone of the solution. Unlike word processing formats that are incompatible across different hardware and software systems, SGML can move across platforms transparently. The Pinnacles members envisioned an environment where different groups within a company would be able to use whatever system is right for their functions. "They are going to create the *same* data," Tommie observes. "But they are going to get there by very different processes — and what process they choose is very dependent on the corporate culture."

Over the summer of 1993 the Peaks held five workshops, one at each of the four member companies and a final reconciliation workshop that all the participants attended. The schedule was grueling. The team would do several days of preparations before each workshop, run the workshop for a full week, then immediately follow up with two or three days of reviews. By November, however, the analysis phase was complete.

TURNING DOCUMENTS INTO DATABASES

Tommie Usdin says, "I'd like to say at the end of workshop 5 we had turned all the mud into bricks. But it turned out that there were more than enough open questions that had to be left for the future. That's how complex this information is." Nevertheless, they had plenty to work on. Over the next three months, ATLIS formalized the definitions and relationships that had emerged from the workshops into Draft Standard PCIS 1.0, a collection of four SGML DTDs[2] describing datasheets, application notes, data books, and miscellaneous documents.

The SGML structure of PCIS 1.0 includes a novel concept that the team calls "source/reflection." Jeff Barton explains it this way: "A Pinnacles document is like a small database. There is one place in a Pinnacles document — the source section — where you can put a characteristic like 'output voltage' along with everything you know about it: its definition, standard symbol, minimum, maximum, and tested value, and so on. Anyplace in the document that you want to show a value, you "reflect" it by putting in an element that points back to the source."

Source/reflection will improve both the accuracy and the cost of maintaining semiconductor data. With word processors, the only way an engineer could put information about characteristics into a datasheet was to actually type it in. Statements such as "$V_{CC} = MIL$" or "The maximum value of V_{CC} is MIL under nominal conditions" quickly spread throughout the documentation. Finding and changing statements when their value changed had to be done by hand. Connections, values, and their physical terminals on the chip are some of the first pieces of information engineers describe, and they change frequently throughout the design cycle of the chip. Datasheets and data books quickly reach a size where keeping the characteristic data up to date becomes a difficult task. Source/reflection will allow the actual values, descriptions, and so on, to be stored in one place. Changing the value in the source section will ensure that the value is correct throughout the body of the documentation.

Source/reflection has another major benefit as well. It can be used to include more information in the electronic documents without making the final document enormously bigger.

---

2 DTDs, or document type definitions, are described in Chapter 1.

THE BENEFITS

Although the implementation of PCIS systems just recently began, the member companies already feel that the investment was worth it. They know the processes their engineers go through collecting, developing, and publishing information about their products — which is something they didn't know before. Jeff Barton says that "Within the first 60 days we learned enough about our information that Pinnacles paid for itself, *even if* nothing else ever happened." Pat O'Sullivan concurs. "As a result of the Pinnacles workshops, we have seen enough improvements in the way we produce documents to make the whole project worthwhile."

The member companies — and other semiconductor companies outside the original group as well — have begun to prototype PCIS internally, and some of the first results have appeared on the World Wide Web. Although Pinnacles was started long before the Web got hot, the Peaks were well prepared with rational plans of action when the first wave of Web enthusiasm hit their companies. Tommie Usdin says that "The process of putting up information on the Web was managed by the right people at the right place in the organization — instead of being driven by the first engineer who put up a Web page." "People said, 'Wow, it's amazing how you guys anticipated this,'" adds Tom Jeffrey. "We didn't set out to develop an HTML-aware application, but because HTML is an SGML document type, when the Web became popular, we discovered that it was a trivial process to get from our SGML into HTML."

Several Pinnacles members have made available in PCIS SGML on their Web sites. National Semiconductor, Philips, and Hitachi are implementing a Web-based, object-oriented search program named Krakatoa™ from Cadis Corporation to provide parameter-based searching of their data books (see Figure 7–3). "One primary thing customers want," Bob Yencha explains, "is to be able to look for products by parametric data. If Delco called up looking for stuff to use in an antilock braking system, we used to say 'Well, take these 23 volumes and start looking through them.' Now, they can do a search on our documents that says 'Show me all the ASICs that have automotive applications' and let the computer do the walking."

Although Pinnacles started before the Web got hot, the Peaks were prepared with plans of action when it hit their companies. People said 'Wow, it's amazing how you guys anticipated this.'

—Tom Jeffrey

National also sees this as a way to substantially increase the number of prospects for their products. Because data books are so expensive to print, they were sent only to those considered most likely to purchase the product. National estimates that before the Web, it was reaching only 10% of its potential customers. Now the data is available to all of them.

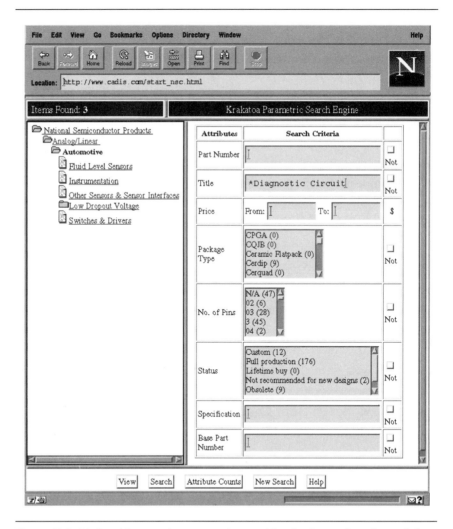

Figure 7–3. National has made parametric searching for its semiconductor information possible over the Web. Krakatoa™ screen courtesy of *Cadis Corporation*.

The Peaks are also working with SGML tool vendors to develop a new generation of authoring software that leverages the PCIS approach to information. These tools will be very different from today's word processors. The requirements for the tools are stretching everyone's conceptual understanding of what an authoring tool should do. Elaine Brennan of ATLIS Consulting says, "Engineers don't think hierarchically, the way the information ultimately gets organized and presented. They think about connections, about how different parts of the device talk to each other or to the outside world, and they learn things in clumps. They need tools that will let them keep what they know together — even though something in-between won't be known for six or seven months. They need tools that reflect their thought processes — not tools that expect them to modify their thought processes to fit what the tool is capable of doing!"

Engineers need tools that will let them keep what they know together — even though some-thing in-between won't be known for six to seven months

—Elaine Brennan

Pat O'Sullivan recalls, "We had a design session in which we prototyped a Pinnacles authoring tool to get the user's require-ments. When we put it in front of technical writers and marketing engineers, they got really excited about what they could do. Now they are going back to the design engineers and telling them, 'We're going to be using this tool — you are probably going to want to use it too.' They're helping us with the sales job."

In January of 1994, the Peaks ran a live demonstration before an audience of 100 at National that showed just how powerful this new approach could be. The theoretical minimum time from start to fin-ish for a new datasheet was three days. But the real average turned out to be more like 90 to 120 days. Bob Yencha describes what happened:

"We took a data sheet that had been converted from our pro-prietary format into SGML and did real-time edits using an SGML editing tool running on a Macintosh computer. To prove this was not smoke and mirrors, we took the requested changes from the audience. We saved the document to a PC file server and then opened it in a different SGML editor running on a UNIX system. The audience could see that all the new edits were there, and that the file had been opened without any kind of file conversion."

"We solicited more edits and saved the file back to the server. At this point we started two parallel processes. We sent the file off via an ISDN line to a printer in Chicago that had an automatic composition system set up to do page layout. While this was happening, we created an online version of the datasheet using another SGML tool. We demonstrated how the electronic version had automatically generated table of contents, hyperlinks, and so on. Just as we were wrapping up the presentation, the printer began kicking out the finished pages from Chicago. The total round-trip time from Mac to UNIX to online and print was 25 minutes!"

In industries like semiconductors, where companies develop products in partnership with one another, rely on strategic vendors for subcomponents, and attempt to customize their products for ever-smaller market segments in ever shorter time frames, success is going to depend on their ability to seamlessly share and exchange product information. The members of the Pinnacles initiative — Hitachi, Intel, National Semiconductor, Philips Semiconductors, and Texas Instruments, not to mention new member companies joining the initiative today — have recognized the challenge and they are taking steps to address it. They are beginning the process of building systems to support what the folks at Intel are calling "The seamless flow of information from creator to consumer." The semiconductor industry may be at the leading edge of the information explosion, but there are lessons in their response for all of us to learn.

CHAPTER 8

SGML Initiatives in Other Industries

*The United States IRS has used SGML for both its forms
and publications since the late 1980s.*

The semiconductor industry may be the champ when it comes to information overload, but it is not the only one where companies realize they have an information-management problem. Defense, publishing, news, commercial aviation, automobile manufacturing, and telecommunications are other examples of industries that have established information standards built on SGML. In each case, SGML is being adopted to speed the flow of information through their businesses.

Governments around the world also use SGML for a broad range of purposes. Many of the federal and state initiatives to better manage the development of legislation and regulations are built on an SGML foundation. The Utah state courts use a simple SGML application to support electronic filing of all case-related documents, replacing a manual, paper-shuffling process that took days with an automated process that takes minutes. The United States Internal Revenue Service has used SGML for both its forms and publications since the late 1980s; you can download SGML versions of IRS documents from the Service's World Wide Web site. Both the European and the U.S. Patent Offices have adopted SGML to improve their ability to handle application approvals and distribution. The list of U.S., European, and Asian government agencies using SGML for their internal information is extensive. And the Securities and Exchange Commission's EDGAR initiative, which requires almost all filings with the SEC to take place electronically, is based on an SGML definition of the information found in SEC forms.

In fact, so many SGML initiatives are underway that to review them all in any depth would require another book. But the following list will provide you with some brief descriptions:

- **CALS** ("Commerce At Light Speed," also known as "Continuous Acquisition and Life-cycle Support") is the original SGML industry initiative. First published in 1985 (even before SGML was formally adopted as an ISO Standard), CALS is a set of standards covering text, graphics, and other media that is meant to streamline the movement of defense-systems information from the contractor to the military. CALS is replacing increasingly unwieldy paper-bound document sets with sophisticated EDI (electronic data interchange) methodologies. The Sikorsky Aircraft case study is an example of CALS in action.

- **ISO 12083: the Electronic Publishing Standard** is an international standard based on SGML DTDs originally developed by the Association of American Publishers (AAP). ISO 12083 is an information standard developed to help the publishing industry use manuscripts for many different types of output, not just paper. Major contributors to ISO 12083 include EPSIG, the Electronic Publishing Special Interest Group, a collaboration of the Graphic Communications Association Research Institute (GCARI), the AAP, and McAffe & McAdam, Ltd.

- **UTF, the Universal Text Format** is an SGML application jointly developed by The Newspaper Association of America (NAA) and the International Press Telecommunications Council (IPTC). The standard was developed to make news articles easier to use in today's increasingly heterogeneous world of news publishing where articles — or parts of articles — may be printed in a newspaper, sent out over a news wire, used on radio or television, and even published on the World Wide Web.

- **ATA Specification No. 2100** is the Air Transport Association's standard for digital aircraft technical information. The goal of ATA 2100 is to make it easier and less expensive for aircraft manufacturers and the commercial air carriers to share and manage things like engine maintenance manuals, service bulletins, and operating manuals. This is no small challenge in an industry where the major airlines spend several *billion* dollars on maintenance each year, and where the document sets not only can total over 100,000 printed pages but also are "specific to the tail number" — which is to say, customized for each and every plane.

- **SAE J2008** is a group of standards developed by the Society of Automotive Engineers (SAE) to help automobile manufacturers meet the goverment's mandate for making emissions-related automotive service information more accessible. Originally, the SAE expected J2008 to be mandated by legislation, but that didn't happen. Instead, companies began adopting it for business reasons. OEMs in the automotive industry are recognizing that there is an economic advantage to be had from storing and managing their information in a form that everybody agrees upon; it makes it easier for the vendors to deliver product information to the auto maker, and much easier for the auto maker to put the information to use. The auto industry is forecast to be one of the leading vertical markets for SGML and related technologies in the years ahead.

- **T2008** is J2008's counterpart in the trucking industry. T2008 was developed by the American Trucking Association.

- **TIM (Telecommunications Industry Markup)** is the Telecommunications Industry Forum's (TCIF) Information Products Interchange standard. Telecommunications equipment —

switches, terminals, and so on — are another of those types of products that require lots of supporting information to use properly, and where all the industry players are doing it differently. Until the TCIF/IPI, the only medium everyone had in common was paper. By defining an electronic standard for the information *on* that paper, the TCIF has moved to support information exchange in an industry with very diverse publishing technologies.

THE SEC'S EDGAR

The SEC accepts the electronic equivalent of between 10 and 12 million pages annually and makes them available to the public in electronic form within 24 hours.

If your company is publicly traded in the United States, then there is one SGML initiative on this list that directly affects you no matter what line of business you are in: the Security and Exchange Commission's *Electronic Data Gathering Analysis and Retrieval* project, more commonly known as EDGAR.

Founded in 1933 in the wake of the stock-market crash of 1929, one of the key missions of the United States Securities and Exchange Commission (SEC) is to act as the clearing house for information about public companies' business and financial condition. The assumption is that in a free and open market, the investing public must have equal access to critical information if they are to have faith in the essential fairness of the market and be able to make informed decisions about investments.

To accomplish this, the SEC requires all publicly-traded companies and certain other financial entities to file a variety of forms, either annually or as part of a specific financial event such as a public stock offering. Over 15,000 organizations file forms, some quite lengthy, with the SEC every year.

This turns out to be a lot of paper. The SEC maintains public reading rooms where these documents are made available, but the task of wading through thousands upon thousands of documents looking for specific information tends to belie the notion of "timely information, publicly available."

In the 1980s, the SEC began experimenting with ways to submit required forms electronically. The idea from the beginning was to build a centralized database of SEC filings that could be made generally — and inexpensively — available to the public, so that anyone with access to a computer and a modem could quickly search for and retrieve any document filed with the commission. In May 1996 that goal was achieved. After a three-year, congressionally mandated phase-in period, the SEC began requiring that all submissions be done electronically. Now, through EDGAR, the SEC accepts the electronic equivalent of between 10 and 12 million pages annually and makes them available to the public in electronic form within 24 hours. Consumers of this information can finally have what the SEC has long sought to provide — near-immediate access to SEC submissions.

At the heart of EDGAR is an SGML DTD that defines the information required in SEC forms. The SGML definitions are extremely precise, defining elements for everything from the filer's corporate information and the form's effective date of filing to nuggets of financial information like accumulated appreciation/depreciation, commercial paper obligations, or investments held for sale. At the same time, the relationship of the information elements to one another is extremely loose, so that virtually any company's style of writing can be accommodated in the filing.

Where companies used to make a business out of searching through all that paper for you, other companies are now jumping in to offer enhancements to EDGAR's basic data. Because the information elements in a filing can be identified so precisely, these companies can add substantial value to the raw filing data very efficiently. For example, some companies offer watchdog services that will automatically notify you when a company on your hot list files a document with the SEC. Others are linking the data from EDGAR filings with commentary and annotations from professional analysts — a kind of "SEC meets Monday night football" service.

Today, most companies' EDGAR filings are being handled for them by their financial printers. For about $200 to $300 per document, these printers tag and submit the filing for you. While the additional cost is nominal, as companies begin to discover the *internal* advantages and efficiencies of having their financial information in a universal format, they will begin to develop systems that allow them to produce their EDGAR filings at the push of a button, almost as an afterthought.

Any where companies recognize they have problems managing document-based material, they discover SGML.

It seems that any where companies recognize that they have problems developing, managing, sharing, and leveraging document-based material, sooner or later they discover SGML. In an increasingly information-based economy, the real asset value of a corporation is going to reside as much in its intellectual property as in its products. But that "intellectual capital" cannot be fully exploited if the intelligence behind the content is locked away inside proprietary file formats, unavailable to programs that could use it for purposes beyond simple printing. Yet that's the problem with today's format-oriented word processors; trying to get at the valuable content inside their files is like trying to eat soup without opening the can. Each of the industry initiatives described here implicitly or explicitly recognizes that problem, and each has adopted SGML as a key component of the solution.

CHAPTER 9

Lessons for Your Future: Learning from the Case Studies

They recognized that the truly valuable resource they were creating was their information, not the paper it was printed on.

Grolier, Mobil, Sybase, Sikorsky — every organization profiled in this book made a decision to protect its investment in document-based information by storing it in a standardized, universal form — a form that could capture more of the author's meaning along with the text, a form that could improve the productivity of their experts while shortening the production cycle, and a form immune to the expensive data-conversion costs that inevitably accompany "software revolutions." Steve Goodman put it this way: "Sybase wants to be able to move with technology, not be locked into one vendor's solution." Richard Weich observed that "Everybody wants open markets and freedom of choice. But in the publishing market, people buy into the vendor-specific systems and they end up driving themselves into a corner where they are trapped by the cost of conversion." Cyndie Cooper said, "You finally get tired of converting your data over and over and you ask yourself, 'If we only had to convert it one more time, what format would we use?' And SGML is the obvious choice."

In each case, the proximate cause, the motivation, the strategic and tactical business goal the organization faced were different. Yet in each case the recognition was the same. Every enterprise profiled in this book recognized that solving its business problem meant gaining control over the content of key sets of documents. And each chose to solve its problem by adopting the Standard Generalized Markup Language — SGML — as the backbone of its technical solution.

In some of these cases SGML was the only solution that could have worked. SGML is the only way to satisfy the semiconductor industry's need to create information that can reliably travel across all the different computers and programs used throughout the industry. SGML is the only way Grolier could achieve the kind of fine-grained access to the content of their encyclopedias that they required.

In other cases, arguably they could have solved the problem using this or the other vendor's shrink-wrapped proprietary solution. Certainly, plenty of companies choose closed, vendor-specific products over open, vendor-independent solutions every day. Sybase had more than one choice for publishing tech manuals on CD-ROM. Mobil could have settled on the desktop-publishing-based system they had bought from another oil company.

But these organizations made a strategic decision as well as a tactical one in building their solutions. They chose to solve today's problem in a way that opened the door to tomorrow's opportunities. *They recognized that the truly valuable resource they were creating was their information,* not the paper it was printed on. In so doing, they moved that information out of the realm of word processors, Web-page editors, and the other format-oriented programs that keep it trapped forever in one output format or another. They moved it into a realm of precise, structure-oriented representation that allows them to use it again and again, in a variety of ways for a variety of audiences.

I am driving home one night listening to a song from the '70s on the radio when it dawns on me that we take this kind of freedom for granted in other areas. I can listen to this song on the radio, on tape, on a compact disk, or on the original record album that still sits on a bookshelf at home. I can find the song in a "Hits of the '70s" anthology. Thanks to the magic of multitrack tape recording, I could sing along to the instruments-only version at a karaoke club (were I so inclined). Somewhere this song is being used as background music in a TV commercial or a department store. The music industry can afford to put this song — a song that is over 25 years old, by the way — out there and make money off it over and over again because the song itself is recorded in a standard way that everybody understands and knows how to use.

This isn't true when it comes to the information we put into documents. I have diskettes in my desk drawer that are only three years old, yet I can't open the documents stored on them because I no longer have a copy of the word processor that created them. Even if I can get the text itself out of the files — and there are programs that will help me do that — all the formatting would be lost. I can play a 25-year-old rock song on my computer, but I can't open a 3-year-old word processing file.

The information we create as documents *can* be intellectual resources as standardized and exploitable as a song heard on the radio. But we must choose to treat them as an asset of the organization instead of a throwaway by-product of our *real* business, whatever it may be. As Alfred Elkerbout of Philips said of the semiconductor industry, "Today, we are moving from documentation as a necessary evil to documentation as an information asset that is an integral part of the product." When you make that kind of mental shift, you start to look at your information in a whole new light.

WHAT DO THE CASE STUDIES HAVE IN COMMON?

At Sikorsky, the driving force behind change was the rising cost of producing helicopter documentation, a cost that kept increasing even though much of the material had been published before. At Grolier, it was the need to move from an annual update cycle to "right-now" maintenance of their encyclopedias — comprising one of the largest and most complexly interwoven bodies of information in existence. At Sybase, it was the desire to switch from truckloads of paper to joint paper and CD-ROM publishing without driving costs and production times through the roof or irritating customers. At Mobil, it was the desire to get control of unnecessary gold-plated extras that were being added to the specifications for offshore oil rigs. And in the semiconductor industry, it was the sheer volume of information being produced during product design, overwhelming the ability of engineers and technical writers to keep up.

The business problem each organization solved was different. The technical solutions each organization used were different. The benefits each organization realized were different. But all of these case studies have several key details in common. Looking at these commonalities can help us recognize the opportunities to make better use of our own information assets.

ALL WERE CHAMPIONED BY PEOPLE WHO COULD SEE "THE BIG PICTURE"

All of these projects were initiated or championed by people high enough in the organization to see the life cycle of their information, from the time it was created to the time it reached its consumers. Because their span of vision encompassed different operations, they could see the inefficiencies, the lost opportunities, the hidden costs incurred in moving that information through the organization and out to its users. And they could do something about what they saw.

Larry Lorimer of Grolier saw what was happening when files prepared for the print version of the encyclopedia went over to the electronic publishing division — the electronic group was typing the cuts made for the paper edition back into the electronic one. Richard Weich of Sikorsky saw that the technical publications, training, and logistics support groups — the three primary producers of technical information — were each researching, writing, and updating the same information.

Disconnects between one department's use of a set of documents and another's are common in most organizations today. Investments in computers and systems for producing documents are still made, by and large, at the department level. The investments are part of the department's budget, and the choices are made with the department's mission in mind. Rarely are the needs of the rest of the enterprise taken into account. From the department's perspective, tools that make it easier to produce polished reports, presentations, or manuals without having to go through other departments (such as art or page composition) look like a smart move — especially in organizations where the department will be charged back for the other groups' time.

Investments in systems for producing documents are made, by and large, at the department level. Rarely are needs of the rest of the enterprise taken into account.

But personal productivity can come at the expense of the productivity of the organization as a whole. The uses for information continue long after it has left the hands of the group that created it. Documents go to customers and also to customer service. They form the basis for quality assurance and testing. They get published on CD-ROMs, commercial online services, or the company Web site. If the output of that enhanced, personally more productive writer is not data that can be fed into different processes and put immediately to use by other groups — and the format-oriented output of most word processing and desktop publishing programs usually isn't — then that output is having a negative effect on overall productivity. It is driving up the company's overall costs and compromising the effectiveness of other groups who make use of the information.

Rarely do the people in one department see the problems that their output creates for those in other departments. Bob Yencha of National

Semiconductor observed that "People who create information often see what they do at their desk as the end of the process; they don't conceive of anything else happening to that document once they are finished with it."

And rarely do the people in higher-level management positions see the problems, because the costs of these disconnects do not show up on the balance sheet. The cost-accounting and other reporting systems that managers rely on to track the performance of the business give the cost of operations, not the cost of processes. They don't show the expenses that are incurred when, for example, one department gets documents from another and then has to rework them significantly before they can be put to use.

Nevertheless, those costs are there. And they are soaking up time and money that could be put to other, more valuable uses every day. Departments, quite rightly, will always look for the best solution to what they understand to be their mission. To look at your organization's information life cycle and recognize where production processes are not working smoothly takes a broader vision. The second part of this chapter has some suggestions about how you can get more perspective for yourself.

ALL WERE INITIATED BY PEOPLE WHO WERE EXPERTS ON THEIR INFORMATION

Few of the projects described in the case studies were initiated by technology experts, but all were initiated by people who were experts on their *information*. Here's why that matters.

Over the past few years, the business use of computers has subtly switched gears. It has shifted from being a means to automate back-office operations (its earliest applications) to being a lever for achieving strategic advantage. Automating back-office operations was largely a technical problem. It could be done by using a computer to rebuild the processes that were already there. Minor insights into process improvements could provide major returns in improved productivity, decreased costs, and so on.

Much of that job is done. Forward-looking organizations are focused on using computers to provide new products and services to their customers, or to significantly improve coordination and communication among internal groups. They are looking to computers to help achieve strategic goals. "The real value of information has shifted from recording to realizing; from recording the past to realizing the future," says Kurt Conrad, president of The Sagebrush Group and a student of the ways that organizations use information and knowledge. "The challenge today is to see the future possibilities offered by fundamentally enabling technologies. Then you can get both business and technical camps mobilized and pulling together."

Envisioning the possibilities begins with understanding how your organization works now, and that means understanding your information. It means understanding what people inside your organization need to know, when they need to know it, and how they communicate with each other. It means delivering accurate and timely information about your products and services to your customers. It means identifying roadblocks to communicating and sharing information.

The key challenge for organizations pursuing this vision is to build systems that can take information created with a diverse collection of hardware and software and make it broadly available to the people who need it. Accomplishing that task takes more than technical wizardry (although such talents are certainly important). It first requires a carefully articulated business problem to be solved, and that takes imagination. Far before it becomes a technical problem, it's a vision thing — the ability to visualize an exciting and more valuable future capability.

So you don't have to be steeped in technology to understand what needs to be done. It's far more important that you do just what you already do every day: articulate the strategic goal, define the vision of a better future. Richard Weich of Sikorsky said, "I still consider myself a computer illiterate." Richard believed that being *too* familiar with the capabilities of the technology can limit your imagination to what you think the technology can do. Instead of starting with a definition of the strategic goal, you risk starting with a definition of what is technically feasible.

The database market has come a long way down this road already. Database technology moved ahead quickly because databases themselves — stores of information for accounting, sales, personnel, etc. — have been perceived from the beginning to be important corporate assets. Customer demand drove market maturity. It is time to recognize that the document-based information your organization generates has lagged behind and move it along as well.

They recognized that software will change — these days, faster than ever — but information sticks around for a long time. They chose to protect what is really valuable.

ALL LOOKED PAST THE SOFTWARE AND FOCUSED ON THE VALUE OF THE INFORMATION ITSELF

In each of the case studies, the participants placed a high value on using open standards instead of vendor-proprietary solutions. Let's put that point another way: they all placed value on the investment in their information, not on their investment in software. They all recognized that software will change — these days, faster than ever — but information sticks around for a long time. They chose to protect what is really valuable — their information — from ongoing changes in hardware and software.

This is important. Many people equate *technology* with *products* — computers and software programs that do something useful. This makes sense, of course, because products are the expression of technology. Products take smart ideas and turn them into reality. There are thousands of computer programs on the market that help get complex jobs done — from photo retouching or mapping to architectural stress analysis or financial modeling.

But there is a downside to equating the concepts of technology exclusively with this vendor's product or that. The makers of computer hardware and software have a powerful economic incentive to do things their way; to use data formats that they develop and own rather than universal, public standards that have been created by organizations like the International Standards Organization (ISO) or the American National Standards Institute (ANSI). One reason is efficiency; product vendors can claim that, by optimizing the form of the data, they can make their products faster and more efficient.

But another reason is purely economic. When you store your information in a product's proprietary data format, then you have created a substantial barrier against switching to the competitor who comes along with a better product. That barrier? The cost of converting your data.

This isn't small change; data conversion is one of the major expenses involved in moving from one vendor's product to another's. Converting 100,000 pages in one desktop publishing format to another can cost up to $2 to $3 per page, according to David Silverman of Innodata Corporation, a leading data-conversion company. That's for routine material. "The costs per page tend to go up as the number of pages to be converted goes down," David adds. "And if those pages contain more complicated content, such as chemical formulas, mathematical equations, foreign-language characters, or complex tables, the cost of manual cleanup and quality control can be enormous."

Faced with a bill like that, can you choose the best product that solves your business problem? Not necessarily. You have to factor the cost of data conversion into your decision. And that cost can kill your enthusiasm for an otherwise terrific product in a hurry. Even if a new publishing system has capabilities that you could use right now, when your current vendor promises, "Just wait — we'll have something even better in six months" you will probably resign yourself to waiting — and hoping that he comes through.

Many companies claim that their data format is *the standard*. Companies fall all over themselves, even give stuff away for free, trying to make their format "the standard in the industry." Why? Because once they own the acknowledged standard, they own that hunk of the market. They may claim their standard is "open" because they publish its specification, but the key test of whether or not something is a genuine open standard is the question, "Can they change it any time they want to?" If the answer is yes, then they can make your information obsolete with the next release of their product. Don't think it hasn't happened to companies before.

You are not likely to see those costs reflected on your balance sheet. Few organizations can reliably measure what it costs to create and manage documents, or what they get for that investment.

The organizations profiled in this book, and many others, learned that lesson a long time ago. Mark Gross, president of Data Conversion Laboratories, was one of the first to specialize in data-conversion services. Mark has seen the impact that software and hardware "revolutions" have on corporate information archives for a long time. "None of us knows what the next technology is going to be. You can only be sure that the answer today will be different in six months," he says. "The organizations who are getting serious about their data are converting to SGML. It's about 75% of our business."

IS THIS REALLY A BILLION DOLLAR SECRET?

I said at the beginning of the book that SGML is obviously not a billion dollar secret for any single organization, but that the costs can easily run into the millions. But how can you know for certain? How can you identify the costs within your company?

One thing is sure: you are not likely to see those costs reflected on your budget reports or balance sheets. Despite the fact that more and more of our companies' computing investments are being spent on systems people use to create and manage documents, few organizations can reliably measure what it really costs them to create and manage those documents, or what they get for that investment. The documents are being created, we know that. But there's no reliable way to measure how much duplication of effort is occurring, how much time is lost reformatting or massaging information before it can be used, or whether or not the resulting documents are useful to our customers.

This is partly due to the way cost-accounting systems look at an organization. Cost accounting looks at an organization as a collection of operating centers. It adds up the expenses of those operations to show you the overall cost of the enterprise. It takes for granted that the work that is being done has to be done.

But creating and using information — particularly document-based information — is a process that crosses department and operating boundaries all the time, and the activities in one area have an impact on costs in others. Cost accounting can show the expense of any one component of that process. It can, for example, show how much technical publications spent on a product manual or how much legal spent on a contract. But it cannot relate the costs in one area to activities in another. It cannot show how much time a tech pubs writer had to spend reformatting input he got from project engineering because they use a different system. It cannot show how much time a lawyer had to spend figuring out which were the final agreed-to-be-accepted changes after a complex contract negotiation.

These extra costs are also due to the nature of the documents themselves. The format-oriented output of traditional publishing software does not lend itself well to being managed systematically. A computer cannot be programmed to handle the files produced by these programs as collections of information elements. They can only be treated as blobs of amorphous data. It is difficult, if not impossible, to build systems that can check and verify the contents of these files, store them as collections of reusable, revisable components, provide audit trails and authentication, or apply security controls to their contents. Workflow and document-management systems can be built to attach some of this information to the outside of a file, but the contents of the file itself are unavailable to help out.

If you want to see the true cost of creating, managing, delivering, *and using* all that information, if you want to determine its impact on your company's business, then you have to look beyond the balance sheets and examine the way the information works its way through the enterprise; you have to look at its whole life cycle. You must identify those information flows that are most vital and/or most costly to your business, then follow them through from start to finish.

Intel put a summer intern on the job; you could do the same. And there are obvious places to look for hidden costs and lost opportunities:

- **Where information crosses organizational boundaries**

  Information becomes useful only when it crosses a boundary, whether the boundary is between one department and another, or between the company and the customer. But if substantial reworking has to be done in the process, it adds to the debit side of your ledger.

  The members of the Pinnacles Initiative — Hitachi, Intel, National Semiconductor, Philips Semiconductors, and Texas Instruments — saw that in action. They discovered that, between the time engineers starting producing information about a new chip and the time the information reached their customers, the content was being retyped four or more times. The information about a semiconductor's functions could not flow smoothly through the mixed computing environments that exist in these companies.

  Grolier experienced it, too. Under their old system, editors were cutting text to fit copy to the encyclopedia pages — and then the electronic publishing group was typing the content back in again for the CD-ROM version. The two groups, with their different requirements, could not share a common body of content.

You don't have to be a cutting-edge technology firm or a big publisher to be struggling with these problems. If you have analysts, engineers, lawyers, writers, or other knowledge workers who must exchange information to keep your business going, then you may well find they have problems reusing each other's information. How much would, say, a 10% reduction in their productivity cost you? These are professional people whose knowledge and expertise makes a substantial contribution to your business. What is the cost of their inability to seamlessly share and exchange information? It is a waste of time and effort that could be spent creating value for the company.

■ Where information is exchanged with key vendors or customers

The same rule that applies internally can apply externally as well. If your important vendors receive documents that perform a substantially similar function in different forms from different departments or groups, it takes them additional time to decipher them, understand their content, and act on it. It reduces the learning curve from one project or contract to the next.

Mobil had this experience. Their contractors were used to receiving bid documents for construction projects in a different form from each engineering center. After Mobil began using the EDEP system, they began getting documents that followed a consistent model. They report that this reduced both the time it took them to prepare a bid and the overall project costs.

The same thing applies to customers. When different groups within your company send out documents that contain substantially the same information, but each with a different look and feel, do you look like one company, or lots of little companies? And what is the impact on your reputation when information in those documents is inconsistent or even contradictory?

Sikorsky found this out. After they reengineered their technical documentation system using SGML, the improvement in quality and accuracy in their documentation was significant enough to draw recognition and praise from their customers. Their error rate had not been bad before the new system was put in use, but afterward it nearly vanished.

■ **Where information is published in different forms**

Sybase had decided that they must publish electronically if they were to satisfy their customers. Yet they had to have printed documentation available. The question was, how could they do both without driving up costs or delaying the delivery of technical information? They already had over 100 writers producing technical documentation. Adding on a group of electronic publishers, who started working with the output from those writers once they had finished, could easily have added 10% to 20% to their head count and added weeks to their production schedules. Instead, their SGML-based system has enabled them to add online publishing to their existing operation without dramatically increasing their costs or their publishing turnaround.

Many companies are struggling with the problem of how to deliver information over multiple delivery channels. Companies are delivering information via fax-on-demand systems, commercial online services and commercial databases, the World Wide Web, electronic bulletin boards and newswires. Each of the channels requires different data formats, different types of organization and indexing, and different processes for distribution. To make the problem tougher, the reason many companies move to these electronic forms of distribution is that the material changes so frequently that they have to find faster ways to get it to customers. The costs of supporting each additional distribution method add up quickly.

If it takes a corporate communications writer two days to reformat your annual report for the company Web site, and that writer's cost to the company is roughly $35/hour, then you have just invested $560 in your annual report unnecessarily, plus you've lost two days that your writer could have spent creating new material for the company. Not much when taken in isolation. But if you have that cost, then it is likely to be the tip of the iceberg. You undoubtedly are experiencing the same type of expense over and over again with each new bit of information that is made available over more than one distribution channel.

■ **Where similar content is reused in different publications**

Most companies that publish the same, or similar, information in several different documents are rewriting that information over and over again. Legal notices and other standard "boilerplate" copy are just one simple example. Other examples are product descriptions coming from both marketing and engineering, computer software manuals for different versions of the same product, testing procedures in classroom materials and also in the field manual. Often the content is coming out of different departments. They do not have a systematic way to share the information and, even if they try, their efforts are often complicated by differences in the hardware and software they use and the different output formats that they have settled on.

Sikorsky had this problem in the extreme. Three different departments — technical publications, training, and logistics support analysis (LSA) — were independently writing substantially the same information. And, because there was no way to reuse common information, even within a department, each new contract required that supporting technical documentation be prepared from scratch. The SGML system they installed not only enabled them to end their reliance on freelance writers to handle the overflow, it made their existing staff 60% more productive.

But you don't have to be a Sikorsky to have this problem. Does your company have to make widespread use of freelance writers to handle the backlog of writing assignments? Do you have distinct departments publishing information that is substantially the same? What would a 60% increase in productivity translate into in your document-producing organizations?

You can also investigate the costs of not being able to respond to market opportunities quickly, of not being able to keep track of the most current information about a product or service, or of not being able to get information into the hands of your staff and customers quickly. You can investigate the cost of bad (inaccurate, corrupted, or unsanctioned) information in terms of lost customers or reduced customer confidence, or even in terms of your legal liability and regulatory impacts.

As managers of the whole enterprise, we need to look at our organization as a chain of related business activities. If we want to make the most of its potential, then we have to look at the processes as well as the individual costs. We have to see where the movement of information through that chain gets disrupted. As managers of individual operating centers, we need to look at where the information being fed to our organization drives our costs up, and at how the information we deliver to others has the same impact on them.

How much does a design engineer's time cost? A market analyst's? A technical writer's or a corporate counsel's? These are your knowledge workers. They are the most professional, highest-paid people in your organization. How much of their time is spent creating information? How much of their time is spent making use of information they get from others? By giving them the tools to integrate information into their work faster and more smoothly, you give them the tools to make a better contribution to the organization and to accomplish more with their time.

SGML is truly a "Billion Dollar Secret" when the gains to all its users — users like those described in this book — are taken into consideration. And as a title, it is certainly an attention getter. But the costs to your company don't have to be anywhere near that amount to affect your bottom line or your organization's efficiency. Once you start to look at the real costs in your organization, the numbers you find will get your attention far more than the title of this book did.

IS SGML RIGHT FOR YOUR ORGANIZATION?

So we come to the obvious question: "Can *your* organization benefit from incorporating SGML into its content production and management systems?" Before you can answer that question, you must first ask another, more fundamental one. For SGML itself is simply a means to an end. It is an enabling technology that gives you the power to manage and exploit the contents of your documents in a far more precise and reliable way than you could before. The more fundamental question to ask is: "Does your organization produce documents that are key assets and that deserve to be managed as such?" The answer to that question depends on the business you are in and the kinds of information your business generates.

We are all publishers today, no matter what our line of business. For some, information *is* the product. Commercial book and magazine publishers are obvious examples of such businesses, but so are legal firms, management consultants, advertising agencies, reference publishers, and the news media. So are educational institutions, nonprofit organizations, and government agencies. Most large enterprises also have internal organizations devoted to creating and distributing material to employees, suppliers, and customers.

For others — the vast majority of businesses — the product is physical goods. Sikorsky manufactures helicopters. The members of the Pinnacles initiative manufacture semiconductor chips. Mobil produces oil, gas, and industrial chemicals. These companies and many others like them see and understand their business in terms of the products they produce. Yet these companies also find that they are producing large and growing bodies of document-based information as well, much of which is an integral part of their products.

Either way, your organization produces a lot of document-based information, quite possibly more than you realize. Whether you choose to use SGML or not, it is in your best interest to better understand the role of this information in your organization. The rest of this chapter gives you ideas on how to look at your organization's use of document-based information and decide whether SGML has a role to play.

DO YOU WORK WITH KEY DOCUMENTS?

Historically, organizations have lumped everything that looks like a document together in one category and treated them all the same. A big part of the problem we have with document-based information has been caused by trying to take a "one-size-fits-all" approach to creating and managing it. We have been trying to create and manage key document assets using the same sets of tools and techniques that we use for memos, business letters, and press releases.

Not all documents are created equal. Most of the daily crop of documents our organizations produce are of a transient nature. They make a request or answer a question; they announce a meeting or summarize a project. These documents — memos, status reports, and the like — are usually short and simple and intended for one use only. Documents like these do not need to be created, managed, or archived using sophisticated systems. Once they have fulfilled their intended role, they are rarely needed again.

But every enterprise produces some types of documents that are not transient at all. These documents carry strategic, possibly critical, information supporting key activities of the business. They may be procedures that tell our customers how to use the product, or specifications that tell our suppliers precisely what we expect them to deliver. They may be contracts or project plans that spell out commitments, timetables, responsibilities, and deliverables. They may be financial filings or other legal, regulatory documents required by law or as protection against liability.

These are certainly "documents," but they are more than the word normally suggests. They are assets of the organization, the tangible embodiment of intellectual property and collective knowledge that your company and your customers take — or ought to take — very seriously.

How can you recognize documents that fit in this class? They generally have one or more characteristics that distinguish them from their transient brethren. Ask yourself these questions:

- Are they long, complex, and interdependent?
- Are they volatile, subject to ongoing changes?
- Do they have departments dedicated to creating and maintaining them?
- Are they long lived? Do you have to maintain them for an extended period of time, usually measured in years?
- Do they appear to be the bottlenecks that keep products from getting to market or projects from getting off the ground?
- Does their content often get rewritten, in whole or in part, in several related classes of documents?
- Do they cross-reference other documents, both inside and outside the company, extensively?
- Do they cross a number of boundaries in the organization in order to be created, reviewed, approved, and finally used — often more than once?

- Are they in demand? Do they have a big audience? Are they used by large numbers of people both inside and outside the company, and do different groups often use them for different purposes?
- Do they have legal or regulatory ramifications? Could your organization be sued for not having them, or for not keeping them up to date, or for making them available at the wrong time?

If you find yourself answering "yes" to these questions, then the documents in question are *not* optional. You *must* create and maintain them if you want to stay in business. Organizations pour a lot of money into documents like these, into creating them, keeping them accurate and up to date, and getting them out to their customers. Most companies put even more money than they realize into these documents because of all the disconnects and hidden costs that are associated with creating them and using them.

Don't be distressed if you find that your publishing systems look less like information pipelines and more like bucket brigades.

ARE YOU MANAGING YOUR INFORMATION CONTENT, OR ITS PUBLICATION?

Organizations have only recently begun to recognize the fundamental difference between the *content* of a document and its delivery *container* — the publication. According to Larry Warnock of Documentum, Inc., a developer of document-management systems, "Content is the domain of the knowledge workers, the most expensive people in the organization. The container of the content — and that's what a publication really is — is just how you get the content communicated." Larry observes that "Those companies that are focusing on the value of the content — seeing that this is *our* drug formula, *our* clinical data, *our* legal precedent — are realizing the value of taking systematic approaches to their information. They are recognizing that content must be created, but publications should be generated on demand."

A printed and bound report is a publication. A page on your Web site is a publication. A CD-ROM is a publication. You need the publications. But most organizations have focused their resources on building systems that satisfy the demands of publishing, rather than on building systems that capture and protect the investment in their content.

Does your organization fit this profile? Has it lumped simple documents with strategic ones? Does your organization have difficulty taking full advantage of the output of its most professional, most productive people? If you wonder whether you are making the optimum use of strategic document-based information resources, all you need to do is walk around and ask. Here are just a few experiments you can try for yourself:

- Find out whether anyone knows how many published documents your company produces, or even how many different departments engage in publishing information at all. You may be surprised to discover that many groups generate documents, often without realizing that others are engaged in essentially similar tasks.

- Collect a handful of documents, old and new, that your company publishes. Ask for the files that created them. Not the PostScript™ files used to print them — but rather the word processing or desktop publishing files that match those printed documents. Often, so many changes happen between the time the files leave the writer and the time the publication comes off the printing press that no files match what ended up on paper.

- If your company has training and customer support groups as well as documentation teams, find out how much synergy exists between them. Ask how much content their publications have in common. How much do they benefit and leverage each other's expertise? You may well discover that they report to different management, maintain different relationships with customers, and cooperate little if at all. Even where these groups want to collaborate, the types of technical barriers described in this book make information sharing between them difficult if not downright impossible.

- Has your company developed a World Wide Web site? Ask how much it cost to produce. Then ask how much of that is the cost of reformatting or otherwise reworking information that already exists in other documents. Assuming that you can get a dollar figure for that particular task — by no means a given — you have just been handed an example of a hidden cost. If your data had been in SGML, that process could have been automated.

- If your company publishes information in another electronic form, such as CD-ROM or commercial online information service, find out how much extra it takes to reprocess the information. Find out if the material is generated from the same files used to create printed publications or whether the electronic publishing group keeps and updates a separate copy of the information.

Don't be distressed if you find that your publishing systems look less like information pipelines and more like bucket brigades. Most organizations are just beginning to come to grips with these problems. SGML won't solve them all. But it will give you the foundation for taking control of your publishing process. It will provide you with the avenue to the type of standardization that we all take for granted in so many other parts of our businesses. Because you don't manage those problems with tools that treat documents like sheets of paper — you manage them with tools that treat documents like data.

ARE YOU READY TO PROTECT THE VALUE OF YOUR INFORMATION?

I hope I have convinced you that information — more specifically, the information that is created and distributed in the shape of documents — is one of your key corporate assets. And I hope I have convinced you that to make the most of this content — to cost effectively extract the most economic value from it over its lifetime — you need to switch from systems that specialize in producing publications, be they formatted printouts or snazzy homepages, to systems that specialize in producing structured information.

What you do need to do, above all else, is decide that your information is valuable enough to protect it from the ongoing turmoil of technical advance.

The case studies presented in this book are here to convince you that this is not only possible but also the smart move. If they have encouraged you to look at the document-based information your company produces in a new light then they have done their job. I have tried to let these case studies speak for themselves, because the information produced by your company is your asset and your investment, and stories of people like you solving problems you suspect your company may have are far more compelling than an avalanche of statistics from a gaggle of gurus. Nevertheless, the gurus agree. For example, InterConsult's 1993 Study of the SGML market found that spending on SGML products and services was growing at 34% per year. They forecast that the market would reach $1.46 billion by 1998. (Source: "SGML Competitions and Markets, Products and Applications, 1994–1998," InterConsult, Inc., Cambridge, MA.) If companies are spending billions on SGML systems, you have to assume that they must be getting even more billions in savings, new capabilities, and other benefits in return.

The people and companies profiled here were, by and large, pioneers. They made a leap of faith and took advantage of a new opportunity, based on the conviction that the approach to information explicit in SGML — the separation of their information from the programs used to deliver it — made sense. When they adopted SGML, there were not many choices of technology available. They took the chance that the idea was right and technology would follow.

You don't need to be a pioneer to turn your company's information into assets. There are more products on the market today supporting SGML documents than ever before. Many of the mainstream software manufacturers have added SGML capabilities to their products because their customers have demanded it. And there are many approaches to implementing SGML to choose from; you don't need to throw the investments you have already made in document-production systems out the door and start from scratch. Many companies have found that they can put SGML to work by making it part of the systems that they already have.

What you do need to do, above all else, is decide that your information is valuable enough to your organization to protect it from the ongoing turmoil of technical advance. Software changes. Distribution channels multiply. The hot desktop publishing product of three years ago is staid today, and today's favorite will likely be struggling to hold onto its market share two or three years from now. Yesterday, CD-ROM publishing was the high-tech topic. Today it is HTML and the World Wide Web. Tomorrow it will be something else. Interactive user manuals, expert systems, "smart" products, and information tailored to an audience of one are all going to become expected norms by customers. The only absolute that you can count on is that technology and the expectations of your customers will change — and change quickly.

Change can be a source of stress, frustration, and ongoing expense for your company, or it can be a source of opportunity. As a business person, you want your company positioned to identify business opportunities and then move quickly to take advantage of them. You want your company positioned to recognize business problems, then apply the tools to solve them. The opportunity should drive the solution. You should not have to compromise what you deliver to your customers because the materials that you have to work with tie your hands.

Which simply means that your focus should be on the strategy. Let your information-technology people focus on the tools.

You have a unique opportunity as a business leader today. Our economy, indeed our world, is going through one of the most profound transformations in humanity's history. The impact of the computer on our society is as significant as any of the developments that have gone before, and we are in at the beginning. Times like these don't come along very often. And if they are disconcerting because they change so much that we have taken for granted, they are also exciting because they offer possibilities that we never had before. You are in a position to make decisions about how your organization responds to these challenges. You can apply SGML — the billion dollar secret — in your own organization. You can turn document-based information into assets. You just have to decide that the time has come to do so.

Afterword: Finding Out More about SGML

I f this book has convinced you that SGML deserves your organization's immediate attention — and I certainly hope it has — then your next step may well be to put somebody to work investigating how useful it can be in your company, and looking for information on SGML products and services. The case studies in this book have, I hope, given you plenty of ideas about what to look at inside your company. This afterword offers several good starting points for looking into the SGML market itself.

Information about SGML is easy to come by. Books, articles, and other resources grow more plentiful as the standard finds more applications, as more users discover and take advantage of its benefits, and as more product manufacturers respond to their interest by developing tools that make use of it. Not only are there books and magazine articles, but there are also World Wide Web sites where you can find a wealth of information, discuss questions with other users, and download free software.

If you are looking for technical books on the standard itself, there is no better place to start than the books in *The Charles F. Goldfarb Series On Open Information Management.* They are excellent resources for readers at all levels, from the novice to the highly technical professional. These titles are published by Prentice Hall, Upper Saddle River, NJ. As a starting point, anyone who wants to understand the fundamentals of SGML and learn how to use it effectively will want to read *README.1ST: SGML for Writers and*

Editors by Ronald C. Turner, Timothy A. Douglass, and Audrey J. Turner and *Industrial-Strength SGML: An Introduction to Enterprise Publishing* by Truly Donovan.

Another resource that anyone interested in SGML will want to follow is *<TAG>: The Technical Journal of the SGML Community*. Published monthly, *<TAG>* is the only publication devoted exclusively to coverage of SGML. It features articles written by leading industry figures, reports on important events, and product reviews. You can get subscription information by contacting SGML Associates, Inc. at 303-680-0875, or via email at tag@sgml.com.

SOURCES OF INFORMATION ON THE INTERNET

Rich sources of information about SGML are available on the Internet.

- If you are seeking a broad overview of information, case studies, books and magazine articles, industry initiatives, technical information, and more, start with Robin Cover's SGML bibliography, located on the World Wide Web at:

  ```
  http://www.sil.org/sgml/sgml.html
  ```

  Robin's bibliography collects in one place virtually all the available information about SGML. He organizes this material into useful categories and adds brief descriptions of each resource to help you decide whether or not it is relevant. The site has extensive links to other locations on the Web.

- Those involved in the technical implementation of SGML as well as ongoing development of the standard will want to subscribe to comp.text.sgml, the SGML newsgroup. comp.text.sgml is Grand Central Station for SGML expertise. Many of the pioneers and leading practitioners of SGML and related standards can be found on the newsgroup discussing every aspect of the standard and its application at any given time. Nevertheless, they are always willing to take time to help a newcomer with a question.

■ SGML Open, the SGML industry consortium, maintains its Web site at:

> http://www.sgmlopen.org

The site features a number of member-written white papers and case studies, as well as links to the Web sites of the members — including all the key industry players. The SGML Open Web site is one-stop shopping for finding vendors of SGML products and services.

■ Finally, anyone interested in news about SGML should subscribe to the SGML Newswire, an Internet mailing list maintained by Avalanche Development Company, a subsidiary of Interleaf Inc. The Newswire distributes press releases, meeting announcements, brief clippings from recent articles, and other information as it becomes available. The Newswire also periodically publishes its "Hit List" of interesting articles and case studies. To subscribe, simply send an email message to sgmlinfo@avalanche.com and ask to be included on their mailing list.

ORGANIZATIONS INVOLVED WITH SGML

The organizations listed below are primary sources of information about SGML or SGML-related activities.

■ The International Organization for Standards (ISO) is the international body charged with developing and maintaining standards in a broad range of industries and activities. The ISO is the

publisher of the SGML Standard, technically known as ISO
8879:1986. Copies of the standard itself can be purchased directly
from the ISO or from your national standards organizations.

International Organization for Standards
1 Rue de Varembe
Case Postale 56
CH-1211
Geneva 20
Switzerland
Phone: +41 22 242340
Fax: +41 22 333430

- The Graphics Communication Association (GCA) helped initi-
ate the development of SGML in the early 1980s. Today, the
GCA sponsors classes and conferences on SGML, including the
annual SGML, SGML Europe, and SGML Asia conferences.
Through the GCA Research Institute (GCARI) the GCA continues to sponsor research and development of SGML and
related standards.

Graphics Communication Association
Norm Scharpf, President
100 Daingerfield Road
Alexandria, VA 22314-2888
Phone: 703-519-8160
Fax: 703-548-2867
Web: www.gca.org

- SGML Open is the SGML industry consortium. The organization's role encompasses both educational activities and technical
industry initiatives. Members include almost every major product
vendor in the SGML and electronic publishing industries.

SGML Open hosts seminars and educational activities and develops presentations, white papers, and case studies. The technical committee of the organization works to develop standards that address interoperability issues among various vendor products.

Information on the consortium can be found on its World Wide Web page, www.sgmlopen.org, as well as by sending email to execdir@sgmlopen.org.

SGML Open
Robin Tomlin, Executive Director
910 Beaver Grade Road, #3008
Coraopolis, PA 15108
Phone: 205-772-2355
Fax: 205-464-9470
Email: execdir@sgmlopen.org
Web: www.sgmlopen.org

- There are user groups specializing in SGML all over the world, but groups spring into being so quickly that no list can stay up to date for long. The best starting point for information on user groups is the international SGML Users Group.

SGML Users Group
Pamela Gennusa, President
P.O. Box 361
Great Western Way
Swindon, Wiltshire SN5 7BF
United Kingdom
Phone: +44 1793 512515
Fax: +44 1793 512516
Email: plg@dpsl.co.uk

Index

— A —

Activities, 7
Air Transport Association (ATA):
  specification 100, 109
  specification 2100, 175
American National Standards Institute (ANSI), 135, 187
AnswerBaseTM, 80
Application type:
  Grolier, Inc., 44
  Mobil Corporation, 128
  semiconductor industry, 152
  Sikorsky Aircraft Corporation, 98
  Sybase, Inc., 72
Association of American Publishers (AAP), 174
ATA specifications, *See Air Transport Association (ATA)*
ATLIS Consulting, 163-64, 167-68, 171
ATM machines, 11
Attributes, 117-18
"Author amnesty," 87
Automated processing of SGML documents, 57
Autotranslation programs, 94
  See also Foreign-language translation
Avalanche Development Company, 207

— B —

Bar-code scanners, 11
Barton, Jeff, 151, 160, 162, 164, 168, 169
Brennan, Elaine, 171
Busicom, 156
Business challenge:
  Grolier, Inc., 46-48
  Mobil Corporation, 131-32
  semiconductor industry, 156-57
  Sybase, Inc., 74-76
Business use of computers, shift in, 184-85

— C —

CALS ("Commerce At Light Speed), 109, 174
Case studies:
  commonality of, 181-82
  Grolier, Inc., 43-69
  learning from, 179-203
  Mobil Corporation, 127-50
  semiconductor industry, 151-72
  Sikorsky Aircraft Corporation, 97-126
  Sybase, Inc., 71-96
  TypiComp, Inc., 27-41
CD-ROMs, 2, 19, 23
Charles F. Goldfarb Series On Open Information Mgmt, 205
Client/server computing, 74
comp.text.sgml, 206-7
Computer-based training programs (CBTs), 122
Computerization Task Force, Grolier, 48
Computers:
  data analysis by, 18
  and document-based information, 11
  and document creation, 1-2
  and mechanical tasks, 16-17
Conrad, Kurt, 185
Cooper, Cyndie, 51-69, 179
Cover, Robin, SGML bibliography, 206
Cross references, 37, 40, 50, 64
  as hypertext links, 81

— D —

Data:
  characteristics of, 19
  defined, 17-18
  documents versus, 19-22
  predictability of, 19-20
  as raw material, 19
  structure, 19-21
Data analysis, by computers, 18
Databases, 2, 11, 111

fields, 18
  turning documents into, 167-68
Database technology, and market maturity, 186
Data books:
  definition of, 157
  for time-to-market windows, 158-59
Data conversion, cost of, 187
Data format, 11-13, 22, 188
  and desktop publishing programs, 13
  early computing, 11
  and word-processing programs, 13
Desktop publishing programs, 158
  and data format, 13, 56-57
Display filters, 82
Document-based information:
  and the computer, 11
  importance of, 6-10
  writing, 15-17
Document creation:
  new types of documents, 2
  and personal computers, 1-2
  and staff needs, 4
Documents:
  building information products from, 27- 41
  and daily operations, 7
  data versus, 19-22
  and information flows, 4
  and internal processes, 7-8
  productivity dilemma with, 10-15
Document type definition (DTD), 24-25, 112
  definition of, 24
  Grolier, Inc., 60
Donovan, Truly, 206
Douglass, Timothy, 17, 24, 206

— E —

EDEP (Engineering Document Enhancement Program), 137-40
  benefits of, 145
  change-control feature, 143
  cost of, 137-38
  "delete section" option, 141-43
  IHS standards database, use of, 139
  as more than reference book, 141-43
  and Revision Log table, 143
  and SGML, 145-46
  testing of, 139-40
  User's System, 140
  User's System Response Form, 143
EDGAR initiative, Securities and Exchange Com., 174, 176-78
Electronic Data Book Working Group, 159-60, 162
Electronic Data Gathering Analysis and Retrieval project, See EDGAR
Elkerbout, Alfred, 160, 162
EPSIG (Electronic Publishing Special Interest Group), 174
European Patent Offices, and SGML, 173-74
Everest, Hiram Bond, 132
Ewing, Matthew, 132
Executive summary:
  Grolier, Inc., 44
  Mobil Corporation, 128
  semiconductor industry, 152
  Sikorsky Aircraft Corporation, 98
  Sybase, Inc., 72
Expert diagnostic systems, 123-25
  information types required by, 124

— F —

Fact-based data, 2
  changes in chain of processing for, 11
Fields, 18
File incompatibility, 13-15, 19-20
Flagging problems, 57

Foreign-language translation, 94-96
  SGML benefits, 96
Format, 22
— G —
Generalized Markup Language (GML), 23
  design of, 24
  document type definition (DTD), 24
  function of, 23-24
  tags, examples of, 23
Gilbane, Frank, 2, 25-26
Glushko, Bob, 85, 87, 89, 90-92
GML, See Generalized Markup Language (GML)
Goldfarb, Charles F., 23-24
Goodman, Steve, 71, 78-96, 179
Graphic Communications Assn. Research Institute (GCARI), 174
Graphics Communication Association (GCA), 208
Grolier, Inc., 43-69, 182
  Academic American Encyclopedia, 44, 46, 59
    cross references in, 50
  application type, 44
  business challenge, 46-48
  CD-ROM products, 46
  Computerization Task Force, 48
  content:
    customizations/tweaks of, 63
    timeliness/accuracy of, 47-48
  cross references, locating, 64
  data types, improved control over, 67
  document type definition (DTD), 60
  editorial operation, streamlining of, 66-67
  Encyclopedia Americana, 44, 46, 59-61, 63
    cross references in, 50
  Encyclopedia of Science Fiction, 46
  encyclopedia size, 49
  executive summary, 44
  foreign-language characters, handling of, 67-68
  graphics extraction/tracking numbers, 65
  Grolier Electronic Encyclopedia, 44
  Grolier Multimedia Encyclopedia, 46-47, 63
  group, 44
  Guinness Multimedia Disk of Records, 46
  and HTML, 64-66
  interdependencies of articles, managing, 64
  internal training, 61
  manufacturing process, study of, 52-55
  mathematical symbols, handling of, 67-68
  mission statement, 44
  New Book of Knowledge, 44, 46, 59, 67
  objectives:
    defining, 55-56
    taking to the manufacturers, 58
  original database, 45-46
    publishing, 48-51
  payoff, 62-69
  personal compute use, study of, 51-52
  Prehistoria, 46
  premier products, 46
    and international online services, 46-47
  prepress costs, cut in, 66
  pre-SGML methods, 53-55, 64
  Request for Proposal (RFP), 55-58
  SGML, 180
    benefits from adopting, 63-69
    converting pages to, 59-61
    and depth of data, 68-69
    introducing to staff, 62
    as a solution, 56-58
    structure, 59-60
  special punctuation characters, handling of, 67-68
  study group, findings of, 53-55
  symbols, handling of, 67-68
  system:
    article preview function, 62
    implementation of, 61-62

  tearsheets, use of, 51-52
Gross, Mark, 188
— H —
Hitachi America, Ltd., 152, 169, 172
HomeAgainTM, 155
HTML (HyperText Markup Language), 64-66, 94
http://www.sil.org/sgml/sgml.html, 206
— I —
IBM, and GML, 24
Industrial-Strength SGML: An Introduction
    to Enterprise Publishing (Donovan), 206
Information:
  as company resource, 10
  generation of, 4
Information Handling Services (IHS), 139
Information resources, 205-9
  on the Internet, 206-7
  organizations, 207-9
Integrated circuit (IC), 156
Intel Corporation, 152, 153, 156, 166-67, 172
Interactive electronic technical manuals
    (IETMs), 98, 122-23, 125
Interactive programs, 23
Internal processes:
  controlling, 4-6
  and documents, 7-8
International Organization for
    Standardization (ISO), 24, 135-36, 187, 207-8
IRS documents, SGML versions of, 173
ISO 8879:1986, 24
ISO 9000, 4
  certification, 77
ISO 12083, 174
ISO, See International Organization for Standardization (ISO)
— J —
J2008, 175
Jeffrey, Tom, 161, 169
— K —
Ketterer, F., 153
Kiser, Denise, 78, 83
KrakatoaTM (Cadis Corporation), 169, 170
— L —
Lashua, Vane, 53, 65
Lorie, Raymond, 23
Lorimer, Larry, 43, 48-69, 182-83
—M—
McAffe & McAdam, Ltd., 174
Marked sections, 115-17
Mechanical tasks, and computers, 16-17
Mission statement:
  Grolier, Inc., 44
  Mobil Corporation, 128
  semiconductor industry, 152
  Sikorsky Aircraft Corporation, 98
  Sybase, Inc., 72
Mobil Corporation, 127-50, 182
  application type, 128
  bid document, developing, 143-45
  business challenge, 131-32
  E&P engineering guides, 141
  EDEP (Engineering Document Enhancement Program), 137-40
    benefits of, 145
    change-control feature, 143
    cost of, 137-38
    "delete section" option, 141-43
    as more than reference book, 141-43
    and Revision Log table, 143
    and SGML, 145-46
    testing of, 139-40
    use of IHS standards database, 139
    User's System, 140
    User's System Response Form, 143
  engineering guides:
    categories of, 138

number of, 138
workshop, 133
engineering specification automation system (ESAS), 134-35
information content/organization of, 135
engineering specifications, 129
executive summary, 128
Exploration and Producing Technical Center (MEPTEC), 132-37, 140, 143-144, 149
consultation with contractors, 134
engineering guides workshop, 133
group, 128
industry standards documents, purchase of, 139
mission statement, 128
Mobil Technology Company (MTC), 132
new system:
existing solutions, 134
finding a vendor to build, 136-37
open standards, 135-36
project proposal, 134-35
and SGML, 135-37, 180
See also EDEP
payoff, 146-49
capital savings, 147
improved product quality, 147-48
reduced cost of direct engineering supervision, 148-49
reduced "gold-plated engineering," 147
reduced number of redos, 148
site-specific guides, 141
tutorials, 138
Mobil Technology Company (MTC), 132
Moore, Gordon, 157
Mosher, Ed, 23

— N —
National Semiconductor, 152, 169, 172
Networks, 2, 11

— O —
Online services, 23
Online viewer products, 80
O'Sullivan, Pat, 159-60, 162, 166-67, 171

— P—
Paper costs, 1-2
Personal computers, and document creation, 1-2
Personal productivity vs. organizational productivity, 183
Philips Semiconductors, 152, 160, 169, 172
Pinnacles Component Information Standard (PCIS), 163
Pinnacles Group, creation of, 162-63
Plans, 7
Policies/procedures, 7
PostScript, 79
Predictability, of data, 19-20
Prioritizing, 7
Products, equating with technology, 186-87

— R —
Rattanni, Dave, 111
Raw materials, standardizing, 18-19
README.1ST: SGML for Writers and Editors (Turner/Douglass/Turner), 17, 205-6
Reengineering, 4
Reporting and analysis software programs, 11
Reuse of written material, 10, 17
Rubinsky, Yuri, 160

— S —
SAE J2008, 175
Salerno, Joe, 106-7
Sargent, Gary, 127, 132-40, 143, 146
Schedules, 7
Schering-Plough, 155
Securities and Exchange Comm., EDGAR initiative, 174, 176-78
Semiconductor industry, 151-72
application type, 152
authoring process, study of, 166-67

business challenge, 156-57
datasheets, study of, 164-66
documents, turning into databases, 167- 68
Electronic Data Book Working Group, 159-60, 162
ENIAC (Electronic Numerical Integrator and Computer), 153
"ENIAC-on-a-Chip" project, 153-55
executive summary, 152
Hitachi America, Ltd., 152, 169, 172
industry problems in information handling, 155
information explosion, tackling, 153-55
information production, analyzing process of, 163-64
integrated circuit (IC), 156
Intel Corporation, 152, 153, 156, 166- 67, 172
KrakatoaTM, 169, 170
members, 152
mission statement, 152
National Semiconductor, 152, 169, 172
Philips Semiconductors, 152, 160, 169, 172
Pinnacles Component Information Standard (PCIS), 163
benefits of, 169-72
Draft Standard PCIS 1.0, 168
Pinnacles Group, 162-63
workshops, 163-64, 165, 167
and SGML, 161-62, 180
solution, beginnings of, 159-60
source/reflection concept, 168
Texas Instruments Semiconductor Group, 152, 172
Services delivery/requests, 7
SGML:
appearance vs. structure, 57
attributes, 117-18
as billion dollar secret, xvi-xviii
conversion, benefit of, 61
converting libraries into, 59
flagging problems in, 57
at Grolier, Inc., 56-58
information resources, 205-9
marked sections, 115-17
origin of, 24
and predictability, 26
processing of documents, automated, 57
reuse, 58
and Sikorsky Aircraft Corporation, 112
and structure, 26, 244
and Sybase, Inc., 81-83
SGML Associates, Inc., 206
SGML initiatives, 173-78
SGML Newswire, 207
SGML Open, 207, 208-9
SGML Users Group, 209
"Shrink wrapped," use of term, 107-8
Sikorsky Aircraft Corporation, 97-126, 181- 82
application type, 98
and computer-aided-design (CAD) systems, 108
and computer-integrated-manufacturing (CIM) environ., 108
correct granularity, 115
electronic products, 122-25
computer-based training programs (CBTs), 122
expert diagnostic systems, 123-25
interactive electronic technical manuals (IETMs), 122-23, 125
executive summary, 98
"expert authors," 113-14
technological support of, 115-17
group, 98
Interactive Electronic Tech Manuals (IETMs), 98, 122-23, 125
Logistical Support and Analysis (LSA) group, 104, 113-14
mission statement, 98
modules, 115
new system:
eliminated rewrites, 120
impact on organization, 118-19
improved accuracy, 120-21

payoffs, 119-21
    productivity increases, 120
    reduced costs, 121
    time cut by, 120
paste boards step, 100, 120
process problems, 103-5
    different groups with different missions, 104-5
    rewritten text, 103-4
production labor costs, 100
productivity, increases in, 120
reengineering the organization, 113-15
and SGML, 112
    attributes, 117-18
    marked sections, 115-17
solution:
    picking, 111
    search for, 102-3, 105-7
    selling to top management, 107-11
table of contents/index step, 100
Technical Publications Group, 104, 113
Training Group, 104, 113
typesetting step, 100, 120
"write once, use often," 113
Silverman, David, 187
Society of Automotive Engineers (SAE), J2008, 175
Source/reflection concept, 168
Specifications, 7
Standard Generalized Markup Language, See SGML
Standards, 7, 18-19
Structure of data, 19-24
    storing, explicitly, 23
    and WYSIWYG programs, 20-21
Style sheets, 82
Sybase, Inc., 71-96, 182
    AnswerBaseTM, 80
    application type, 72
    business challenge, 74-76
    and CD-ROM publishing, 76-77
    Client-Library/C Programmer's Guide, 76
    and client/server computing, 74
    cost savings, 87
    DB-Library/C Reference Manual, 76
    and delivery issues, 82
    desktop publishing tool vs. SGML authoring tools, 88
    executive summary, 72
    group, 72
    information delivery, changes in, 78
    and ISO 9000/TickIT certification, 77
    mission statement, 72
    new system, 90-92
        building, 83-84
        building the environment for, 88-89
        installation process, 85-86
        and SGML, 81-83
    online publishing solutions, 79-80
        online viewer product, 80
        search program, 80
        send customers printable files, 79
    Open Client and Open Server Common
        Libraries Reference Manual, 76
    Open Client/Server documentation set, 76
    and Passage Systems, 85-87
        SGML syntax with, 86-87
    payoffs, 92-96
        cost reductions, 92-93
        satisfied customers, 93
        technical documentation on the Web, 93-94
        translation cost reductions, 94-96
    Phase I, 87
    Phase II, 88-89
    previewing online versions, 88

and production issues, 82
publication managers committee, goals of, 78
Quick Reference Guides, 82
and SGML, 81-83, 180
    configuration process, 85-86
    converting first set of documents to, 85
    writers' need to learn, 89
standards, corporate commitment to, 76- 77, 84
SyBooks, 73, 87, 90-92
    and customer satisfaction, 93
    reduced production costs for, 92-93
System 11 product line, 93
Tools and Connectivity Troubleshooting Guide, 76
utilities, development of, 90
word-processor style sheets, 82, 86
World Wide Web (WWW), and delivery of updated
    information, 93-94
writers' issues, understanding/supporting, 89-90
Writers' Tools Group, 89
                    — T —
T2008, 175
<TAG>: The Technical Journal of the SGML Community, 206
Technology, equating with products, 186-87
Templates, 82
Texas Instruments Semiconductor Group, 152, 172
TickIT, 77
Time-to-market windows, for databooks, 158- 59
TIM (Telecommunications Industry Markup), 175-76
Total Quality Management (TQM), 4
Turner, Audrey, 17, 24, 206
Turner, Ron, 17, 24, 206
TypiComp, Inc., 27-41
    and SGML, 40-41
    Testbed Information Management System (TIMS), 29-41
        automatic conversions filters problem, 36-38, 40
        benefits of, 30
        cross reference problems, 37, 40
        development team, 33-34
        and FingerTip, 33, 36
        information amassed, 35-36
        misunderstandings about, 39-40
        101st-page paradox, 37-39
        prototype, 31-33
                    — U —
Usdin, Tommie, 163, 164-67, 169
U.S. Patent Offices, and SGML, 173-74
Utah state courts, and SGML, 173
UTF (Universal Text Format), 174-75
                    — V —
Van der Spiegel, J., 153
Visual clues, 22-23
Visual effects, 19-20
    and WYSIWYG programs, 19-20
                    — W —
Weich, Richard, 97, 102-26, 179, 183, 186
Word-processing programs, 158
    and data formats, 13, 56-57
    style sheets, and SGML, 82
World Wide Web (WWW), 2
    and delivery of updated information, 93-94
    and HTML, 64-66
WYSIAYEG, 23
WYSIWCG, 92
WYSIWYG programs:
    SGML-aware versions, 21
    and structure, 20-21
    success of, 22
    and visual effects, 19-20
                    — Y —
Yencha, Bob, 151, 159-60, 162, 166, 169-72, 183-84